Understanding the

G-SPOT

and Female Sexuality

**A 10-Step Guide
for Unleashing the Ultimate in Female Ecstasy**

by Donald L. Hicks

Understanding the G-Spot and Female Sexuality:
A 10-Step Guide for Unleashing the Ultimate in Female Ecstasy

Copyright © 2001, Donald L. Hicks

Cover Photo: SuperStock Inc.

Universal Publishers / uPUBLISH.com

USA / 2001

www.upublish.com/books/hicks.htm

ISBN: 1-58112-657-3 paperback

ISBN: 1-58112-655-7 ebook

Table of Contents

Dedication

This book is dedicated to Arleta, the one person who encouraged me to write. The wife who never complained about the trough I wore in the floor while pacing restlessly back and forth, searching for that elusive word or angle. The woman who never laughed at the bald spots worn above either ear from scratching my head in thought. The one person who had unwavering confidence in my abilities, even when I lacked faith in myself.

Without her patience and understanding, this book would not exist.

Learning the Basics

Does the G-Spot Exist?

You may be wondering if the G-Spot is real.... Does it exist, or is all the "G-Spot hype" just a selling tool for magazine articles or adult novelties? And if the G-Spot does exist, why is it there? Why is it so easily overlooked? What physical purpose does it have? Does the penis touch it during intercourse?

And most importantly, if the G-Spot does exist, how does one find it and coax it from hiding?

This book will answer all of these questions.

You may also wonder about female ejaculations — "squirting" as the phenomena is often called. Is "squirting" merely more sales hype, or are female ejaculations real? And if female ejaculation does occur, why haven't you seen it? Why does it occur? What physical purpose is there for female ejaculations?

If you're wondering about any of these questions, let me take a moment to congratulate you for taking the time to enrich your knowledge and understanding of female sexuality. As you will learn from these pages, the phenomena of the G-Spot and female ejaculations are not new to society. Documented mentions of these enigmas can be traced back through history to as early as Aristotle. And without doubt, millions of people have reached their graves without ever experiencing the joys and pleasures offered by the G-Spot.

The goal of this book is simple. We want you to learn, first-hand, that both G-Spot orgasms and female ejaculation do exist and can be evoked to bring about the ultimate in female ecstasy and sexual enjoyment. More importantly, you'll learn why these two phenomena exist, how they've been overlooked countless times in the past, and the important roles they play in the processes of human reproduction and childbirth.

Through these pages, you'll learn a proven and tested "10-Step technique" that shows you how to find the G-Spot, how to stimulate it, and how to drive your lover crazy with ecstasy. You'll deepen your understanding of the female anatomy while learning new methods of rekindling the romance and sexual excitement in your current relationship.

The G-Spot does exist. Through this book, you can prove it to yourself, and your lover.

What's the big deal about G-Spot orgasms, anyway?

"My lover and I have great sex...why do we need to worry about the G-Spot?"

If you've never seen or experienced a true G-Spot orgasm, imagine for a moment, an orgasm that causes the whole vagina to spasm violently, often contracting so tightly that it literally tries to "force out" your finger or any object in the vagina. And imagine that while these intense contractions are throbbing and pulsing throughout the vagina, the vagina becomes very wet, often literally ejaculating a stream or spurt of fluid with each contraction. Imagine an orgasm that causes such intense ecstasy that even the quietest and most controlled woman will yelp and buck and thrash; one that makes normal "screamers" go dead silent—the scream caught in her throat—a scream that if freed may wake all the neighbors within a five block radius.

And imagine the satisfaction of never having to wonder: "Did she just orgasm? Did she fake it, or was it real?". But instead knowing the instant her orgasm begins by clear physical signs that occur involuntarily and accompany the orgasm.

This is the glory of a G-Spot orgasm.

But we don't want you to take our word for it. We want you to see for yourself.

Here's what a few others had to say:

"I didn't think orgasms like that were real. . . I thought they only existed in romance novels. . ." — B. R.

"It was absolutely the deepest, most wonderful climax I've ever felt! It was like warmth started in my very center and flowed outward all over my body. I loved it!" — L. K.

"I thought I had wet the bed! And then (name withheld) explained what had happened and I could hardly believe it finally happened to me. . . If I have to wash the sheets every day for the rest of my life, it's worth it."— T.J.

"I wanted it to last forever and couldn't stand another second. . . both at the same time. It was the greatest!" — M.J.J.

"After that, I'll never let (name withheld) get away from me! Our love life has never been better. . ." — K. A.

"She used to just lie there and moan through the whole thing. It was frustrating because I never knew when she was orgasming or if she even orgasmed. Thanks to your technique, there's no more guessing..." — T.P.

The Dire Truth
about Conventional Orgasms

While most men can go from "slightly-interested" to "full-ejaculation" and orgasm in an average of 3 to 4 minutes, orgasms for women are often more elusive. On average, a women requires 15 minutes (or longer) of combined foreplay and stimulation before orgasm is achieved. The reward: a clitoral or vaginal orgasm lasting an average duration of 8 to 19 seconds.

In the early 1970's, a detailed nationwide study showed that nearly 12% of women never experienced any type of orgasm! The same study showed that 16% could have an orgasm during intercourse (with the addition of clitoral stimulation) and 19% achieved a rare orgasm through intercourse alone. Only 26% had an orgasm on a regular basis (30% when including those who claimed to have vague "good feelings" in the vagina).

Couple this with the brief 8 to 19 second duration of an average orgasm and you have a very dire picture.

Another segment of the study showed controversy over "clitoral" orgasms vs."vaginal" orgasms. The consensus showed that clitoral orgasms (empty vagina) were largely considered "higher intensity" than orgasms with vaginal penetration—but there was a catch-22 factor. During clitoral stimulation and orgasm, most women felt a strong desire to have an object in the vagina. The problem with this "vaginal craving" was an immediate decrease in pleasure if vaginal penetration was made.

Additional parts of the study concluded orgasm intensities could range from questionable ("was that an orgasm I felt?") to pure ecstasy—but the high-intensity orgasms occurred much less frequently. The study also showed that most women have intercourse for the purpose of sharing emotional intimacy, while another group's primary motivation was to obtain the ever-illusive orgasm. One study showed that about 1/3 of the women studied enjoyed anal penetration while another 1/3 didn't like anal penetration. Another study showed that 21% of women desired daily sex, while 18% —nearly the same amount—were satisfied with sex 3 times per week. Other studies probed masturbation with fingers versus objects, sex with the legs together versus spread, and the preference of different positions during sex.

The relevance of this information is to elucidate the obvious: we are all different and have different tastes and desires in a partner and how we interact with that partner. We have different needs, likes and dislikes. Secondly, it brings to light the sad reality that many women never orgasm, and those who do aren't always satisfied afterwards.

But now there is hope.

Duration in the length of orgasm is one area where the G-Spot leaps ahead.

Unlike the normal vaginal or clitoral orgasm, the G-Spot orgasm lasts not a mere 8 to 19 seconds, but often lasts 45 seconds — with common reports of 2 minute orgasms and rare reports of orgasms lasting between 20 and 40 minutes! One man reported:

"She kept orgasming as long as I was rubbing the spot. It never quit or slowed down. We have a clock radio on our night table and it went on for at least 45 minutes. I know that sounds like an exaggeration, but it's not. I was beginning to think it might harm her in some way if I kept going. And I was ready to explode any minute. Watching her thrash around in ecstasy and feeling how warm and wet her [vagina] was against my fingers was driving me crazy. Her [vagina] kept contracting and squeezing and she felt as tight as a schoolgirl again. It was driving me crazy. I love this G-Spot thing."

A few women have reported needing to stop their partners from continuing stimulation because the pleasure was "excruciating" or "nearly unbearable." One woman stated:

"The anxiety was overwhelming. At first I thought it would never come and when it did, the ecstasy was almost unbearable. It felt so wonderful I couldn't stand it. I thought I might go crazy from the pleasure. I wanted to keep going, but had to stop, both at the same time. And when it was over, I was exhausted and totally satiated. Total bliss doesn't define what I felt. It's not even close."

Beyond driving your lover crazy with long-lasting ecstasy, an additional benefit of G-Spot stimulation may be a reduction in risk for cancer and diseases in the female prostate (also known as Skene's paraurethral glands and ducts). While the occurrence of female prostate cancer is low and seldom fatal, any reduction of risk is still beneficial. According to many alternative health experts and Oriental practices, massaging the prostate can drain toxins and stress. In the book, *The Prostate Miracle, New Natural Therapies That Can Save Your Life*[i], the authors discuss similar means for cleansing the male prostate gland and releasing toxins.

Although the female prostate is smaller than the male counterpart, the two develop from the same embryonic tissue. Because of their similarity, one might hypothesize that stimulation of the female prostate and the corollary release of fluids and cleansing could offer the same benefits as male prostate stimulation. This topic of women's health deserves future research.

The 92% Factor

Using the technique provided in this book, an astounding 92% of our respondents reported success within the first 3 applications of the technique! This percentage includes women who previously considered themselves either non-orgasmic or reported low occurrences of orgasm.

In one survey we conducted, women were instructed to grade "Vaginal", "Clitoral", and "G-Spot" orgasms on a scale of 1 to 10 (with 10 being the "most pleasurable" and 1 being "least pleasurable"). Of the respondents who achieved successful G-Spot orgasms, the average rating was a "10" (One woman claimed it was "*off the chart*")! The average rated clitoral orgasms was an "8" and vaginal orgasms ranked third in pleasure intensity with a "6".

When asked to describe their G-Spot orgasm experience, we commonly received the same four statements within most descriptions:

1. "It was deeper than anything I'd felt before."

2. "It felt very different from previous orgasms."

3. "It was more fulfilling/satisfying than previous orgasms."

4. "It felt 'better', 'more pleasurable', or 'more intense' than other orgasms I've had."

In addition, many women equated the G-Spot orgasm to a "whole body" event, whereas other orgasms were "pelvic". We received many comments about feeling a "heat" that started deep within "their core" and spread throughout their body. Coinciding with this statement, many of the sexual partners (who administered the technique) made comments such as: "she broke out in a sweat afterwards" or "she was drenched and exhausted" or "she threw off the covers".

Many women also reported their first (noticed) "female ejaculation" occurred with the G-Spot orgasm. One re-occurring comment we received was: "I thought I'd wet the bed. . .". We have heard this comment over and over.

While G-Spot orgasms and female ejaculations are separate entities, the two sometimes occur simultaneously. We'll discuss female ejaculation in greater detail, later.

Like finding a half-bloomed rose, you now have a glimpse of the G-Spot's glory. Soon the petals will unfold.

Why Does the G-Spot Exist?

Beyond the intense sexual pleasure the G-Spot is able to produce, new studies are investigating the G-Spot's value in blocking pain during childbirth. In an article titled *Beyond the G-Spot: Recent Research on Female Sexuality*[ii] which appeared in the January 1999 Issue of Psychiatric Annals, authors Whipple and Komisaruk state: ". . . a series of studies has demonstrated that self-stimulation of the anterior wall of the vagina in women produces a significant elevation in pain thresholds. . ." and "we believe childbirth would be more painful without this natural pain-blocking effect...".

This research (which has been replicated by other researchers) shows the G-Spot's value during childbirth. Because of this, we feel that the physical purpose of the G-Spot is:

1. To ease pain during childbirth (as shown by Whipple and Komisaruk).

2. To either enhance or provide sexual pleasure.

By stating "enhance" sexual pleasure, we are referring to "non-direct" G-Spot stimulation. For example, when the penis swells during normal intercourse, the increased girth of the penis may partially stimulate the G-Spot and "boost" a woman's sexual enjoyment to the point she orgasms with her partner. If your lover has ever said anything like: "You started swelling and hitting something up in there that felt great..." you may now understand what was happening. Likely, the partial stimulation of the G-Spot enhanced her sexual pleasure.

By stating "provide" sexual pleasure, we are referring to direct stimulation of the G-Spot. Which, as you will hopefully soon learn, can provide a stand-alone unparalleled source of orgasm.

A Side Order to Go, Please

By following the technique outlined in this book, one can obtain indirect rewards along the way. The Ten-Step system is designed to teach G-Spot understanding and prowess, yet it also incorporates the building blocks for enriching and strengthening relationships." Heightened intimacy" is a good example. We all need a partner with whom we can share our hopes and dreams, our fears and desires, our failures and our triumphs. We need someone to laugh with and someone to help us forget the pressures society heaps on our shoulders. Sharing intimacy and having friends to confide in can be an important element of good emotional health.

"Spontaneous praise" is another suitable example. When we're dating that special someone, praise is a wonderful tool. It's a great way to evoke a smile, a word of thanks, or perhaps even a kiss. We use praise to hint our feelings toward that person by saying "I love *this* about you" or "I love *that* about you". And because of the smile it often evokes, we freely point out our mate's beauties, skills, or whatever qualities we admire in them. They smile, love us for our admiration, and often return a like sentiment.

As the relationship progresses, however, we tend to withdraw from praising our partner and she or he withdraw from praising us. Offering praise becomes similar to giving part of ourselves away: a silent forfeiture of power. It fosters feelings of inadequacy because giving praise somehow makes us feel like "less" and the other person like "more". Beyond that, the lack of received praise begins to gnaw at our own self-worth. We start second-guessing whether our partner still admires the traits she or he once freely applauded. We vow not to venture out on a shaky limb and praise him or her if they no longer praise us. The same praise we once used as a helpful tool has now become a weapon, and we set ourselves up to have a "praise stand-off" with our mate, like two petulant children pretending to be gunslingers.

With the stealth of a snake, a rift has split the ground between us and our partner, widening with the passage of time, until we are separated by an immense void.

But this need not be the case. As we know, the world can be a harsh place. It continually beats us down. At times, the simplest word of encouragement from our mate can bolster and fortify us, giving us the strength to lift our chin and carry on. By recognizing the fact that we need praise, it's easy to understand that our mate needs praise too, in all the same ways. And whom do we want as the source of that praise: ourselves, or a stranger? What does it really cost us to give praise? What might it cost if we don't?

Like most things worthy of pursuit, the rewards you (and your partner) receive along the way to the G-Spot—pleasure, tenderness, open communication, increased sexual awareness and sexual expression—will reflect the effort you extend.

One successful user of the technique had this to say:

". . . Thanks so much for introducing me to the G-Spot and sharing your wealth of sexual know-how. You have no idea how beneficial your time and insightful comments have been in restoring my marriage. Before reading your book, my wife and I were on the brink of separating. Lovemaking had become an unimaginative weekly ritual for us. The fires of romance that once blazed brightly had dwindled to a pile of cool ashes. We spoke to each other only out of necessity and both felt we had grown apart. Now, that has changed. The knowledge you imparted has changed that. By following your suggested steps, the doors of communication re-opened. My wife and I discovered that we still have many common goals; they were just buried underneath the headaches of everyday life. We were both bored in the bedroom and had little desire to cuddle or do anything that might lead to sex. Now, we're like teenage lovers again. Our relationship is renewed. We take walks together, talk openly, and have adventurous sex daily (twice if we can manage). It all started that first night I tried your technique. The seed for new growth was planted. I (we) can't thank you enough. "—G. P.

If your relationship has grown stale and lacks romantic luster, congratulate yourself for purchasing this book. You've taken a positive step toward rekindling the fires of romance. And while buying a book may seem insignificant, remember that knowledge is a powerful tool. Sometimes the smallest spark can set off the largest blaze.

The matches are now in your hand.

Blended Orgasms
A Recipe for Higher Ecstasy

"What are blended orgasms?"

Suppose for a moment that your mate mentally rates a clitoral orgasm as a "7" and a G-Spot orgasm as a "10". What would happen if she felt both of these orgasms at the same time? The answer is simple: she would experience an (off-the chart) blended orgasm.

In the early 1970's, Irving Singer touched upon the concept of "blended" orgasms[iii]. Thereafter, while studying the continuum of orgasmic response and the corresponding nerve pathways, Whipple and Perry validated, defined, and clarified the reality of "Blended Orgasms"[iv].

In layman's terms, blended orgasms are two or more orgasms occurring simultaneously (or in very close rotation). Blended orgasms originate from multiple sources of simulation. For example, if you perform cunnilingus as you stimulate your partner's G-Spot, she may experience a blended "clitoral/G-Spot" orgasm.

While the two obvious sources for blended orgasms are either (1) "stimulation of the clitoris and G-Spot" or (2) "stimulation of the clitoris and vagina", we need not limit our thinking to only these two combinations. An orgasm can originate from a variety of sources. For some women, having the breasts massaged or nuzzled is very pleasurable and can bring about orgasm. For others, petting and necking (with or without breast stimulation) can induce an orgasm. Others reported an orgasm during dreams, while horseback riding, and even while dancing[v]. And for others, mental imagery alone[vi] [vii] (without any physical stimulation) can cultivate orgasm.

Opposite of this, as we discussed in the earlier segment, 12% of women reported never experiencing any type of orgasm. Others reported being able to orgasm through only one type of stimulation, such as clitoral stimulation. Logic would therefore indicate that not all women are likely to experience blended orgasms—unless they find new sources or methods of becoming orgasmic.

We hope the technique you learn from this book will be such a source; a freshly bloomed rose, filled with sweet nectar.

To Orgasm, or Not to Orgasm?

That is the question many people ask themselves during intercourse.

Because you purchased this book, it's highly probable you would enjoy seeing your mate experience a "blended orgasm". And it warrants mentioning here, your display of unselfishness and caring is commendable. However, while the thought of seeing our mate experience a blended G-Spot/clitoral orgasm may be appealing, we must learn to "walk" before we can "run".

As we learn to "walk", the first mental step is learning and accepting that people choose to orgasm. Deciding to orgasm is a personal choice. No one can "give" or "will" another person an orgasm—no more than you could "will" a stranger to remove their clothing.

We each make individual choices concerning "if" or "when" we will achieve orgasm—often without conscious deliberation of the subject. For those who are highly orgasmic, the sheer act of removing clothing (or allowing it to be removed) may mark the decision. For others, the decision may not be concluded until stimulation or coitus is underway and "the waters are tested", often mere seconds before orgasm. Others release their reservations in layers. Like an autumn tree shedding its leaves, they slowly drop inhibitions, as they grow resoundingly secure and comfortable with the relationship. And yet others refuse ever to relinquish control, usually from fear of self-humiliation, or to avoid appearing too "wanton" or "loose".

Along the way to making the decision, there are several determining factors ensconced within the decision-making process. In order to "let go" and orgasm, most people need to feel secure with their partner. We need to feel good about ourselves, safe at the location, and comfortable with what's happening to our bodies.

These factors are more prevalent if we're with a new partner or trying a new experience. While "new" can be exciting, the excitement is fueled by the suspense of not knowing what to expect. And because we don't know what to expect, we reserve judgment until late into the process.

All of this is important to consider as you administer the G-Spot technique. As you may recall, one of the four most common descriptions we receive about the G-Spot experience is: *"It felt very different from previous orgasms"*. Because of this, at some unknown point while you're applying the G-Spot technique, your partner will realize something new and very exciting is happening to her. She will then have to decide whether "to orgasm, or not to orgasm".

Deciding whether or not to reveal the G-Spot technique is up to you. If you tell your mate beforehand of your plans to administer the G-Spot technique, you may set up to be a victim of "orgasm anxiety" (discussed later). On the other hand, if she senses something new and unknown is happening to her (while you're applying the G-Spot technique) she may "hold back" and delay or inhibit the orgasm due to the uncertainty of what she's feeling.

It's a catch-22 situation and you should remember this as you go.

We recommend that you don't initially mention your plan to administer the technique. Instead, be aware that at some point during your administration, she will sense this "new and exciting" wave of pleasure building within her. Watch for the signs of her uncertainty. When you see these signs, begin reassuring her that you know what's occurring and understand it. *("I know what's happening to you. It's okay. I'm here. Just enjoy what you feel")*.

The same thinking holds true with blended orgasms. While we encourage the pursuit of blended orgasms, don't overwhelm her by trying to make the first G-Spot orgasm a "blended G-Spot/clitoral orgasm". Take it one step at a time. After she grows familiar with G-Spot experiences, gaining both confidence and understanding, she'll be better suited (if not eager) to explore the bold world of blended orgasms.

Intimacy 101

The *Merriam-Webster Dictionary* defines the word "intimate" as:

"Marked by very close association, contact, or familiarity; marked by a warm friendship; suggesting informal warmth and privacy; of very private and personal nature."

As illustrated through the above definition, people share intimacy with, not only their lovers or sexual partners, but also with close friends, family members, and even pets.

Since the subject matter of this book deals with inner-couple relationships, most references to "intimate" or "intimacy" refer to the *bonding, topics of private and personal nature,* or the aspects of *carnal knowledge* that occur within a relationship.

This point is being clarified because it's important to acknowledge that intimacy need not be linked to sex. Intimacy is the sharing of one's innermost feelings and thoughts with someone we trust. Not only does it erect temporary buffers to the outside world, it also provides a brief respite from stress. It staves off loneliness and promotes our self-worth. Conversations are "mind-to-mind"; intimacy is "heart-to-heart".

The Phenomenon of Female Ejaculation

Beyond intimacy, one other clarification needs to be made before we start covering the technique. Modern society tends to propel the myth that G-Spot orgasms and female ejaculation are the same occurrence. And while the two often do occur together, it's important to realize they are separate wonders—not one entity.

For simplification, we'll explore this topic through a "question/answer" format:

If G-Spot Orgasms and Female Ejaculation aren't the same, what exactly is "Female Ejaculation"?

Female ejaculation occurs when a women "ejaculates" fluid (usually different than urine) from her urethra during sexual arousal or orgasm.

Where does this fluid come from?

Surrounding the urethra and running to the neck of the bladder lies a network of glands, ducts, and nerves called the "Skene's Paraurethral Glands". As we mentioned earlier, these glands are the female counterparts to the male prostrate. The Skene's Glands are the source of female ejaculate.

If it's not urine, what is this fluid?

The fluid is typically described as "clear" or "milky", having little or no odor, and a sweet taste. However, as with male secretion, the taste may change due to dietary intake or possibly as part of the menstruation cycle[viii].

The primary chemical makeup of the fluid is glucose, fructose, prostate specific antigen (PSA) and prostatic acid phosphatase (PAP)[ix x xi xii]. The fluid may also contain traces of urine[xiii].

Interestingly enough, fructose is one of the components present in male ejaculation. Its primary job is to mobilize the spermatozoa. While it was once believed that male fructose was the sole propellant of spermatozoa, the presence of fructose in female ejaculate would evidence the contrary. Instead of passively waiting for spermatozoa to "swim" to the egg, the female plays an equally active role in the reproduction process by infusing her own fructose and ushering the spermatozoa's movement, thus increasing the probability for successful fertilization.

Because of this, we feel the physical purpose of female ejaculation is to aid in the mobilization of spermatozoa. And while it may not be scientifically proven, it stands to reason that stimulation of the G-Spot and the female prostate may be a beneficial pursuit for couples facing problems with conception.

As another interesting note, early forensic medicine checked rape victims (and/or spots on their clothing) for the presence of acid phosphatase, to prove rape had occurred. Research on female ejaculate has since proven this test has no forensic value since female ejaculation contains acid phosphatase.

What causes female ejaculation?

Since the G-Spot encompasses the Skene's glands and the glands are caressed during G-Spot stimulation, fluid is often released into the urethra as a result of G-Spot stimulation. However, G-Spot stimulation is not the sole source of ejaculation. Some women ejaculate with stimulation of the clitoris[xiv][xv].

Do all women ejaculate?

The evidence is inconclusive on whether all women have the ability to ejaculate. If the presence of fructose is designed to play an important role in reproduction, one might hypothesize that all women should have the ability to ejaculate, barring those with physical anomalies, removed Skene's Glands, disease, or hereditary disorders. However, in some studies researchers did not notice expulsion of fluid during stimulation.

In the *Secrets of Sensual Lovemaking, The Ultimate in Female Ecstasy*, author Leonardi states: *"...a combination of physical technique and psychological security were absolutely necessary in order for a woman to have ejaculatory orgasms."* Many of the accounts in Mr. Leonardi's book indicate the need for a strong emotional bond to be established prior to successful female ejaculations[xvi]. If this is true, it could explain why some laboratory studies fail, whereas others (conducted in a more natural atmosphere) can often succeed, especially those done by researchers who willingly provide "in home" examination or testing.

(As demonstrated in the 10-step technique, we feel emotional bonding is a key ingredient to success).

It has also been hypothesized that, because many woman are reclined during intercourse or stimulation, the fluid is retrograde-ejaculated into the bladder and is later released during urination. In *The G Spot and Other Discoveries About Human Sexuality*, the authors state: *"Some women may experience retrograde ejaculation if the fluid shoots into the bladder rather than out the urethra.* [xvii] *"*. This condition might be characterized by a woman feeling a need to urinate after orgasm, but, when doing so, only releasing a small amount of clear or milky fluid.

Along these lines, Cabello, author of *Female Ejaculation, Myth or Reality*[xviii], tested the hypothesis that all women may ejaculate, but some may retrograde ejaculate and therefore might be unaware of the ejaculation, since the fluid becomes mixed with urine in the bladder and is later released during urination.

Of 212 completed and usable surveys we received in doing research for this guide, 48% of women responding reported either they did not ejaculate or were unsure if they had ejaculated. On the opposite side of the gamut, 5% reported ejaculating before orgasm and 47% reported ejaculating during G-Spot orgasm. Of these 110 women who reported ejaculating, 101 reported the incident was their first known ejaculation. Eight others stated they had ejaculated in the past, while one woman informed us she commonly ejaculates with stimulation of the breasts, clitoris, and vagina.

A 37-year-old (single) woman reported:

"The first time I slept with (name withheld), I thought I'd wet the bed. It was very embarrassing for me because I really loved him and wanted sex to be good for us. And it was good in ways I'd never dreamed of. I've been having orgasms regularly since I was 16 (years old) but nothing like this had ever happened. I've slept with 7 different men and always considered my sex life as 'good' until this orgasm. Now I know what I was missing all those years. This orgasm was very different and so much deeper and better than the ones I've had before. (Name withheld) is a definite keeper. . ."

Another woman reported:

"I didn't know I could ejaculate. I'd heard of other women ejaculating but had no idea that I could do it until my friend applied your technique. It was quite an experience. . ."

Does the ejaculation always occur along with orgasm?

No.

In a study conducted by M. Zaviacic (et al.) in 1998[xix], a group of 10 women were studied who ejaculate through G-Spot stimulation. Of the 10 women, they found that 2 participants ejaculated within the first 1.5 minutes of stimulation, prior to orgasm. Five other participants ejaculated after 4 to 8 minutes of G-Spot stimulation (again prior to orgasm). And the three remaining participants ejaculated with orgasm, after 10 to 15 minutes of G-Spot stimulation.

How much fluid is ejaculated?

This is a controversial topic.

Most scientific studies gauge the average female ejaculation as ranging between "a few drops to one-teaspoonful"— comparable to the average volume of semen ejaculated by males. An example of such appears in *The G Spot and Other Discoveries About Human Sexuality* (recommended reading). The authors state: *"In the cases of female ejaculation observed by Whipple, Perry, and their colleagues, only a few drops to about a quarter of a teaspoon were usually expelled[xx].*

On the opposite side of the spectrum, we have received reports of women "drenching the bed" or producing "copious amounts" of fluid. One man had this to say:

"She left a wet circle about a foot in diameter. We were both amazed at how large the spot was. The sheets were saturated. There was no foul odor. No noticeable odor in fact. But the bed was too drenched to allow comfortable sleep."

Another man said:

"Sometimes it just trickles out of her and sometimes it gushes and leaves a big wet spot. It's great if she's on top because having that warm liquid flow down over my testicles makes me [ejaculate] almost instantly. We don't mind changing the sheets afterwards. It's worth it."

Another stated:

"This milky liquid squirted out of her and splattered between her knees. It left a two-foot long wet streak on the sheets."

And:

"She normally ejaculates between one-half cup to one cup. But the first time [she ejaculated] it was more, maybe a cup-and-a-half."

And:

"About a week after we started using your technique, we bought a plastic mattress liner for our bed. You might want to recommend this to other people, along with buying a couple of extra sets of sheets. Otherwise, the center of the bed gets too wet after a couple nights of fun."

And:

"She literally drenched the bed. When it comes to volume, women put men to shame."

A woman stated:

"I don't mind washing the wet bedclothes every day. This orgasm is worth it."

In Tom Leonardi's *Secrets of Sensual Lovemaking, The Ultimate in Female Ecstasy*, several of the interview subjects indicated "large amounts of the fluid". On page 114, one such subject stated: *"And the insides of her thighs were dripping wet. . ."* Another said: *"She came and she squirted. It hit me in the arm. It hit my arm and I'm not sure where the rest of it went. . . . from my forearm all the way up near my elbow."*

In describing the event, Leonardi states on page 57: *"At the very least, her hot liquid will quickly seep out of her, running down her buttocks and off her body. But most likely, the liquid will physically fly from her vagina—2, 4, 8, even 12 or more inches from her."*

The "larger volume" conjecture might also be supported by a custom called *kachapati*, which was practiced by the Batoro tribe of Uganda, Africa. According to a personal communication from anthropologist Phil Kilbraten[xxi], the *kachapati* was a rite of passage for young women emerging from puberty into womanhood. Before these young women were eligible for marriage, the older women of the village taught them how to ejaculate. The term *kachapati* literally means to "spray the walls". One might conclude, in order to "spray the walls", a significant amount of fluid would need to be expelled.

So how is it that skilled researchers report only a "teaspoonful" or less while many people claim it's more?

Considering that most female ejaculations occur in dimly lit or near-dark conditions—and are coupled with the excitement of lovemaking (and perhaps the novelty of a first-time event)—we feel that some estimates of the fluid amount are exaggerated or over-estimated. In example, if you take a teaspoon of water and dump it onto a flat non-absorbent surface, the water will form a circle approximately 3.5 inches in diameter. If you repeat the same experiment, but cover the hard surface with an absorbent piece of material, (such as a cotton bed sheet), the teaspoon of water will soak outward and form a circle 8 inches in diameter. Since many mattresses are treated with stain-resistant protections such as ScotchGuard™ and are covered with heavy upholstery that resists permeation, the bed linens often absorb (and diffuse) the bulk of the liquid. Also, because air can travel through the weave of many bed linens, the heat quickly dissipates and causes the area to feel cool and saturated.

Some researchers feel that Urinary Stress Incontinence (USI) may also play a role, as urine is sometimes released "as" or "along with" ejaculate, thus increasing the volume. However, other researchers argue against this, claiming that—because it is physiologically impossible for a man to urinate at the moment of orgasm—the same likely holds true for women. (This latter argument does not account for women ejaculating urine prior to orgasm).

What's it all mean?

While the jury is still out on certain aspects of female ejaculation, advancing research has played a valuable role in the advancement and betterment of women's health. In the past, many women who described "ejaculations" to their physicians were misdiagnosed with USI and were often directed to undergo "corrective surgery" for the "problem". Beyond the embarrassment brought on by their "shameful condition", some women faced the wrath of a spouse who believed his wife urinated on him during intercourse! As one can see, the plight of these women was unpleasant. Fortunately, due to groundbreaking research by Addiego, Holoman, Komisaruk, Molcan, Perry, Whipple, Zaviacic, Zaviaciova, and other great researchers, acceptance of female ejaculation is coming about.

Some Healthy Considerations

Most medical doctors agree that the therapeutic values of intercourse far outweigh the risks, provided "safer sex" practices are followed. During intercourse, muscles can receive exercise. Stress, stored in the muscle tissue, is released from the body. In addition, the physical stimulation and the movement during both foreplay and intercourse force the heart to beat faster and breathing to increase. This causes oxygen-enriched blood to be spread throughout the body, replenishing cells and feeding muscles.

We've all likely heard the office water-fountain jokes that "so-and-so must have gotten lucky last night" because he or she seems to glow and is unusually cheerful. These statements may have medical validity since, like all forms of exercise, the release of stress can brighten our disposition and help make the world less gloomy and foreboding.

When engaging in intercourse, readers are urged to practice "safer sex". If you're not familiar with "safer sex" practices, there are a host of informative books available, such as: *Safe Encounters: How Women Can Say Yes to Pleasure and No to Unsafe Sex* (B. Whipple and G. Ogden, McGraw Hill, 1989) or *Safe Sex in a Dangerous World* (A.Ulene, Vintage Books, 1987). Your family physician is also a good learning source. Many physicians have educational pamphlets available or can provide information on sexually transmitted diseases (STDs) and their avoidance.

Contrary to popular belief, the risk of heart attack occurring during sexual activity is very low. In a study performed with patients who have suffered heart problems[xxii], only .09% cited sexual activity as the triggering factor. Sexual orgasm has been compared to "about the same energy required for climbing two flights of stairs. . . or walking on a treadmill at 3 to 4 miles per hour"[xxiii]. Compared to many other activities, the risk is low.

If you have a history of heart-related illnesses or other medical condition (such as blood pressure or blood sugar irregularities), you should check with your physician to learn safe guidelines. Also, know your partner's health. It's a wise practice to discuss his/her health status—any sexual diseases and any other health concerns—before engaging in intercourse.

A Brief History of the G-Spot

There's an adage that states: "To know where you're going, it's helpful to know where you've been." This statement holds true with the G-Spot. By cultivating a deeper knowledge and understanding of the G-Spot's history, you increase your odds for success using our ten-step technique.

We owe a great debt to the visionaries of our world. Not only to those who live today, but to those who have come and gone. Throughout time, gallant individuals have seen beyond common perceptions and silently shouldered the duty of discovering truth. In many cases, after enduring countless hours of research to validate their cause, these selfless individuals stepped forth buoyantly to declare their findings—only to have their hopes bludgeoned by ridiculing peers.

Christopher Columbus might serve as a fitting example. At age 14, he became a sailor. For many years, he studied known maps of the world; likely doubting the world was "flat" as was commonly believed. Later, as his theories of a "round world" manifested themselves, he conferred with European scholars (who also believed the world was round). Gaining conviction, he set forth to prove his theory. Yet when he announced plans to sail to the East Indies by crossing the Atlantic toward the west, he was persecuted by "flat thinking" peers.

As we all know, Columbus sailed and prevailed. His ship did not fall off the edge of a flat Earth and into oblivion. And although he never reached his original destination, he discovered something greater in the process—a bold new uncharted world.

Like most great discoveries, the G-Spot and the reality of female ejaculation both follow a similar history. Throughout history, brave and dutiful visionaries have arisen time-after-time to confirm the existence of this uncharted sexual continent, often bearing the ridicule of skeptical peers in the process. Aristotle may be one of the earliest recorded examples by observing that women expel fluid during orgasm. In the seventeenth century, a Dutch anatomist Regnier de Graaf described a "female 'prostatae' or corpus glandulosum" which expulsed fluid, enhanced libido, and caused pleasure. In his findings, he stated: "The function of the 'prostatae' is to generate pituitoserous juice which makes women more libidinous. . ." and "the discharge from the female 'prostatae' causes as much pleasure as does that from the male 'prostatae'.[xxiv] "

Long after Regnier de Graaf's work, Alexander Skene, M. D., George Caldwell, M. D. , John W. Huffman, M. D., Samuel Berkow, M. D., and several others individually studied these glands and/or female ejaculations and released their own findings.

At the end of World War II, a German gynecologist and obstetrician named Ernst Gräfenberg collaborated with an American gynecologist and obstetrician by the name of Robert L. Dickinson, M. D. In 1950, Gräfenburg wrote about "...an erotic zone could always be demonstrated on the anterior wall of the vagina along the course of the urethra...[xxv]". According to the findings, this erogenous zone swelled when stimulated and "swells out greatly at the end of orgasm."

In the 1970's, while treating women suffering from Urinary Stress Incontinence (USI), John D. Perry, Ph.D, and Beverly Whipple, R. N., Ph.D, made an important discovery that led them to the G-Spot. Typically, women suffering from USI have weak or atrophied pelvic muscles. The strength of these muscles can be measured through biofeedback and can be strengthened by teaching women Kegel exercises (a technique for strengthening the Pubococcygeus or "PC" muscle). However, Perry and Whipple discovered that some of the women who supposedly suffered from USI had very strong pelvic muscles. Furthermore, these same women with strong pelvic muscles often stated the only time they (accidentally) lost fluid through their urethra was during intercourse.

Much like Columbus's epic journey, setting forth for the Indies and discovering America instead, Dr. Perry and Dr.

Whipple discovered their own land of milk and honey, which they aptly named "The Gräfenburg Spot" in honor of Dr. Ernst Gräfenburg's early research.

At the 1980 national meeting of the American Association of Sex Educators, Counselors and Therapists, and the 1980 international meeting of the Society for the Scientific Study of Sex, Perry and Whipple presented their findings about the G-Spot and Female Ejaculation. Later, in 1982, along with Alice Kahn Ladas, they published a book explaining The Gräfenburg Spot, Female Ejaculation, the Importance of Healthy Pelvic Muscles, and New Understandings of the Human Orgasm. This popular long-standing book is titled *The G Spot and Other Discoveries About Human Sexuality* and is still in print as of this writing.

Since the release of *The G Spot and Other Discoveries About Human Sexuality*, more has been learned about the G-Spot and female ejaculations. As each new doorway to knowledge is unlocked and opened, we find yet more another doorway awaiting. The more we learn, the more mysteries await us. History unfolds while no one is watching.

The Technique

Let's get started!

Okay. Now that you know a little about the G-Spot, you're probably wondering how you can test the G-Spot technique first-hand.

Let me commend you if you've read through this far and haven't skipped ahead. One of the most frequent complaints women voice about poor lovers is having a partner with "vaginal objective". This "vaginal marksman" wants to kiss once or twice, perhaps then fondle the breasts, then skip any other delays and move right toward the clitoris or vagina. If you've taken the time to read this far, you're likely not a "Vaginal Marksman". (They are now reading "step 10" and will have to back up, re-read, and likely will *never* get this straight. A year from now they'll be the ones responsible for rumors that the G-Spot doesn't exist). You, on the other hand, will find the truth since you have displayed the two most important attributes to actually being successful in helping your lover achieve a G-Spot orgasm. These are: patience and self-control.

Stop for a moment and look at the big picture in logical terms: if the G-Spot orgasm were something *easy* to achieve and could be stumbled upon, nearly every woman on the planet would know what it is and how to do it. Right? Most would have found this spot (as they do their clitoris, during exploratory masturbation), and would be enjoying its pleasures. But as we know, nothing could be further from the truth. Even in this day and age, the G-Spot is still arcane, obscure, misunderstood, and a topic of curiosity.

As evidence of this, we will look at an internet educational service called KISISS (Kinsey Institute Sexuality Information Service for Students). KISISS allows Indiana University students to ask questions about sex in an anonymous fashion. After each question is answered, both the question and answer are posted for other site users to read. Interestingly enough, at the time of this writing, the #1 most frequently *read* question is: *"What is the G-Spot and Where Can I Find it?[xxvi]"* . The sheer fact that college university students (and visitors) read this question more than any other question lends us insight. Clearly, it shows that the G-Spot is still a mystery.

Like dark ships passing on a night sea, most people repeatedly overlook the G-Spot. As many women pass through life, they mature, explore their own bodies, masturbate, have intercourse, bear children, and often never find their own G-Spot. All the same time, the partners who shared in the lovemaking have also overlooked this special spot.

Beyond this, up until two decades ago, many of the very doctors who examine women daily (gynecologists and obstetricians) were unsure of the G-Spot's existence.

In the defense of these physicians, we should consider that (1) the G-Spot cannot be seen without dissection of the anterior vagina wall and (2) it is virtually unnoticeable until stimulated. Since gynecologists and obstetricians are not in the practice of stimulating their patients, it stands to reason they would fail to notice the spot.

With all this in mind, if you truly want to find the elusive G-Spot and help your partner feel the *absolute best* orgasm she's ever felt—a spasming, screaming-and-thrashing-in-ecstasy G-Spot orgasm—you'll need to have patience and self-control.

Follow the 10 Steps implicitly. After you learn and become familiar with the G-Spot orgasm, you'll be able to use the technique very quickly and effectively to help your lover produce results much of the time. But like any worthwhile endeavor, the technique takes practice. The more you do it, the quicker you'll learn to identify certain "signs" given by the female body that allow you to move on to the next step of the process.

The same is true of your partner. If you have a steady sex partner, after she loses her G-Spot virginity she will also learn to read her body signs and will be able to hit the G-Spot climax sooner, and in a wide variety of positions.

Step 1
Priming

Although it's possible to help a woman achieve a G-Spot orgasm on the first sexual encounter, the surest bet is with steady partners who are familiar and comfortable together. This is because of *emotional* qualities. In order to fully *let go,* many women need to feel safe, loved, and secure with their partners' sexual prowess and understanding.

Recommendation number one: As was said earlier, it's wise not to mention the G-Spot orgasm to your partner. If you tell her you want to "try something new" you'll be fostering expectations in her that may be counter-productive when you actually get down to lovemaking. She'll feel the need to "perform" without understanding the details. Therefore, she will be apprehensive and edgy—when it's helpful to be exactly the opposite: *relaxed and comfortable.*

Instead of telling your lover about your covert plan, set up the opportunity to "show" her. Sit down with your lover and tell her that you'd love to take her out for dinner or a movie, then return home and spend the evening making *slow passionate love.* Be sure to mention the second part of this plan so your lover doesn't get the wrong impression—that the two of you are going to spend the evening *out* together. This will do two things for you. One, your lover will appreciate your candor and the romance of the gesture; two, it will prime her for lovemaking. If your relationship is fair or better, she'll probably be thinking about the lovemaking long before you order supper or choose a movie.

Beyond this preparation, be sure to groom yourself prior to your date. Because much of this technique involves stimulation of the vagina, be sure your fingernails are short, clean, and smooth to avoid damaging the soft tissues of her body. Wear your favorite cologne. Look and feel your best.

Step 2
Foreplay

After you wine and dine her, talk about old times and those to come, perhaps give her flowers, brush the spinach out of your teeth from dinner, maybe slow dance in the living room and eventually work your way to the bedroom, be sure to remind her of how beautiful she is and how much you enjoy being with her. Boost the intimacy. Talk to her. Remember that for many women, foreplay is mainly emotional. Spend lots of time on the emotional bonding. Strengthen your relationship and bond with her.

Step 3
More Foreplay

Most likely, with a few more kisses, some light petting, and additional compliments, the two of you will be stripping each other as if your clothes are on fire—falling into the bed together as if it were the only pool of water in the world. And this is when you need to gently take control. If this is your steady partner and you've primed her the week before your "date", she'll likely be wet and ready to fall into your standard lovemaking. Seize control by telling her you want to "take it slow" this time. Remind her that you want to make slow love to her—that you want to spend some time pleasing and savoring *her* and making *her* feel loved. She'll love you for that. Ask her to lie back and make herself comfortable. Remind her that you love her and remind her how beautiful you think she is. If she has beautiful breasts, tell her so. If it's her eyes, her long legs, or her full sensual lips that you like, tell her so. Praise is a key element within any relationship. It costs nothing to give but can be priceless when received. It helps us maintain a healthy image and self-worth while making us feel respected, desirable, and loved. If you love your partner, praise her. Tell her what you love about her; not just her physical beauties, but her emotional qualities, skills, or whatever it is you truly admire.

By doing this, you're promoting a deep sense of intimacy and comfort while keeping her aroused. Kiss her. Nibble on her lips. Kiss her throat, the lobe of her ears, her eyelids—all of which are very erotic and arousing spots for the majority of women.

In the case of most women, by the time you've spent a few minutes kissing all about her face, nibbling the lips, kissing the eyelids, perhaps blowing in her ear, and dragging your lips over her neck and down to her shoulders, you'll probably notice her beginning to inch upward or pressing your face toward her breasts. . . arching her back. If she's forward, she may seek you out with her hand or guide your hand to her breast. She may even tell you she wants you—but don't sell off the million-dollar orgasm that cheaply. A critical element here is keeping *all* your attention, physical and emotional, focused at breast level or above.

Step 4
Teasing

So here you are, in bed together, probably naked by this point, very aroused and ready. You've (both) been thinking about this moment ever since you first mentioned the evening out. This is the part where both patience and self-control are beginning to come into play—don't sell yourself short and give in!

Lavish her with kisses. If she enjoys having her neck kissed, by all means oblige. If she enjoys breast stimulation, nuzzle and fondle and tease her breasts. At this point you can "bend" the rule of focusing all attention at the breast level (and above) by rubbing her stomach. This is an important step in the arousal process. The purpose of this step is to increase blood flow in the pelvic area. Work your hand back and forth across her stomach and down her abdomen *very slowly*. You don't want her to think you're targeting the vulva, so move slowly and randomly until you've reached the area just above the pubic hairline. Absolutely DON'T drop your hand any lower—even if she tries to move it there—even if she tells you she wants you and starts pulling you toward her.

The reason you don't want to touch any lower than the abdomen (yet) is because it breaks the bond you're working to build. Some women have experienced the "vagina marksman" and may be emotionally turned off when interest is transferred to the vagina (if done too soon). When this occurs, it often signifies the "end" of the bonding process and the "beginning" of sex. It can flick as quickly as a light switch. The mist of enchantment lifts.

Continue to nuzzle her breasts, kiss her, nibble at her neck, or whatever shows your love. Your goal is to continue increasing the emotional bond between you, and she will unconsciously give you signs as the strength of the bond deepens. Remember— you're about to provide the stimulus for an orgasm that is unlike anything she's ever felt. In order to reach it, she'll be slowly transferring her trust to you. She'll need to feel cherished, safe, and adored in order to do so without holding back.

As you nuzzle at her breasts, kiss her neck, nibble her ears, or whatever it is that turns her on, you are watching for two "go ahead" signs before moving to step five. The first is the most important. You must continue stimulation until she is virtually smashing your head into her chest, breathing heavily, tugging at you as if she's trying to pull you inside her. Once you become aware of this, start watching (or sensing) for the second sign: movements in her hips. The hips never lie. . . and you want her thrusting them upward. If she's not thrusting, arching, or twisting her hips, she's not ready. So continue nuzzling and sucking at her breasts or otherwise stimulating her until her hips move. If need be, move your hand a little lower on her abdomen to brush the upper edge of the pubic hair as you rub. Before long, both of these signs will come.

Step 5
The "Go Ahead" Sign

Once you have the two "go ahead" signs of arching hips and tugging, absolutely don't break contact with her breasts, chest or face. Keep your head and face at chest level or above. This gives the unspoken message that "you're still with her"—not merely moving on to focus on her vagina and get your next lay.

With the hand you've been using to massage her abdomen, slowly trace down to rub her upper and inner thighs—again, without touching the vagina and setting off the "vagina marks-man" alarm. If you'd like, reach around and squeeze the lower half of either buttock in a teasing way. Massage the muscles gently; working the flesh actually tugs at the edge of the vulva, helping to open the labia and helping her become more ready and wanton. This massage also increases blood flow in the pelvis, arousing and heightening sensitivity.

Trace your fingers up and down her thighs, provocatively circling her "magic triangle". Brushing the edges will ensure her hips continue to thrust.

Above all, remember to focus on her and hold the emotional bond you've established.

Step 6
Hovering

By now she should be thrusting her hips wantonly and moving in a way to actually encourage you to touch her vagina. If she's bold, she may try to massage herself or try to guide your hand (or other part) to the area. However, don't let her. If necessary remind her lovingly that you want to spend more time just touching and savoring her. If she wants to massage herself, encourage her to massage her breasts. Moreover, encourage her simply to just lie back and enjoy.

Your next step will be to move your hand above her womanhood and hover it there, just brushing the tips of the pubic hair. If she's really aroused, this will drive her absolutely crazy. She'll sense your hand and the heat of your hand and should impulsively arch her hips toward your hand. Expect this reaction and raise your hand to avoid contact.

While hovering, you may even tug at the hair lightly. You need not tease her in this way for more than 2 or 3 minutes, but be sure to allow your hand to hover above her womanhood long enough for her to show some type of acknowledgment—even if that's only a moan.

Many women harbor inhibitions about being verbal or displaying their sexual needs or desire. The underlying significance of the "hovering" is two-fold. Not only does it increase your lover's arousal, but it also encourages her to *react* and helps to break through any inhibitions she may be struggling with. It should be abundantly clear that you are deliberately (almost mercilessly) teasing her, searching for a reaction, and this gives her a justifiable *reason* to react without compromising her ego or sacrificing dignity. You've compelled, almost forced, her to react. And for many women, once they have reacted the first time and break the barrier, it's easier and acceptable to react again.

After you've hovered and received a reaction, allow your fingers to trace up and down the flesh on either side of her vagina. By saying "flesh", we do not mean the labia but rather the mounds on either side of the vulva. Touch it *very lightly*. This is an extension of the tease and should further fuel the fires of arousal.

Continue this for a while and slowly change the feather-light touches into a soft massage. Few people realize there are muscles on either side of the vaginal opening, so take a little time and gently massage these muscles, relaxing them.

After you've massaged these muscles for a moment, trace her vagina with your fingers, using a finger on either side of her vagina to lightly pull back and spread open the labia. The labia are a very sensitive and erogenous area, yet many women report they are overlooked during lovemaking. So spend a little time here, flattening the genital lips and tracing them with your fingertips. Gently tug at them and spread them open. This sense of the vagina being "open" will often trigger a high "vaginal craving", and she'll want that void filled.

If you'd like, you may even stroke the clitoris lightly—but don't linger there as the clitoris can be very disruptive to first-time G-Spot orgasms. If you've thought of the clitoris as the primary stimulus point for a woman, you'll want to re-train your thinking. From this point on, think of the G-Spot as the main stimulation and the clitoris as either a "booster" or a secondary stimulus. Remember that the women polled report that G-Spot orgasms are significantly more intense than clitoral orgasms, both in duration and fulfillment.

As we discussed earlier, "blended orgasms" are an exception to this rule and will certainly warrant future exploration. But for tonight, this special first night, we'll avoid the clitoris unless she really needs an extra boost.

In some ways, the G-Spot and the clitoris are like internal/external counterparts. G-Spot virgins, who have spent a lifetime thinking of their clitoris as their primary stimulation, may get so involved trying to give themselves a clitoral orgasm that they lose track of the G-Spot stimulation you're trying to build. While it has not been scientifically proven, our belief is that "single-task" persons can only focus on one form of internal stimulation. . .just as they can only focus on one form of external stimulus at a time. Logical thinking would lead to the conclusion that "multi-taskers" are more likely to succeed at blended orgasms.

Whether or not this is the case, we advise you try to keep your lover away from her own clitoris for this night. Touch it enough to tease, and then move on.

Bear in mind through this whole process, never break contact with her breasts or above. . . returning frequently to kiss her lips and ward off her advances if she tries to pull you onto her.

Step 7
Locating her G-Spot

By now there should be no doubt she's ready. She should be moaning (at least quietly), thrashing her hips, arching her back, and urging you on. And as you finally dip your finger into that moist warm wetness, your patience and self-control will be tested to their maximum endurance. But don't give up. . . you're almost there!

Slide your finger into her very slowly—dipping in very shallow at first to allow your finger to become moist—pulling out and dipping in again. As you do this, dip a little deeper each time, keeping light pressure on the front wall of the vagina—all the while be careful not to scratch those sensitive folds of velvet with a fingernail.

When touching a woman, many lovers make the error of plunging a finger as deeply into the vagina as possible and wiggling the member around, not realizing that aside from the hidden G-Spot, most of the sensitive nerves lie within the first two inches of the vagina's throat. Hence, the adage: It's not what you've got but how you use it. So don't make the error of plunging. Your goal here is to tantalize the outer nerve endings while allowing your finger to become sufficiently lubricated to visit hidden depths.

If your partner is not well lubricated, you may want to use a suitable lubricant. Her being "dry" does not mean she is not aroused. Diet, hormonal levels, medications, and menstrual cycle can all affect vaginal lubrication. Wetness is not a valid gauge of arousal.

Finally, slide your index finger into her, skimming the upper wall. This is the critical process of locating the G-Spot, so while you're still kissing her, teasing her nipples or sucking her breasts, concentrate for a moment on what your finger encounters.

Study the following diagram. This may help you better understand the location of the G-Spot when the time comes.

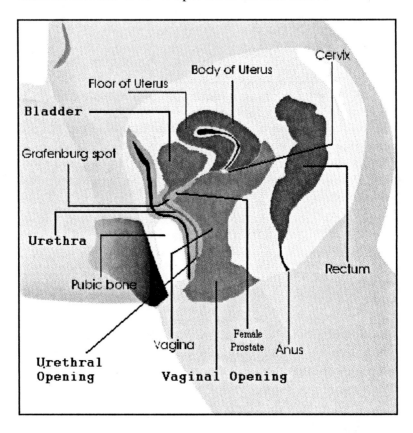

With most women, about one-and-one-half inches inside, you'll feel a slightly textured area of skin (it feels somewhat the same as the roof of your mouth). Just beyond this textured area is the G-Spot, hidden in what feels like a "valley". If you go too far and pass the G-Spot, you'll feel a smooth "plateau" that is flat for an inch or two, then curves inward toward the cervix opening (which is also a very erotic spot if caressed lightly—although it is hard to reach).

If you go too far and reach this plateau, back up to the bottom of the "valley" and rub the down-slope between the valley and the edge of the textured area.

In most cases, the G-Spot feels like a small bean or a very small nipple. At other times it can't be sensed at all. Just like breasts or nipples, some women have small G-Spots and others have larger ones. (The former is especially true of post-menopausal women).

Once you've found the G-Spot (or are in the vicinity where it should be, if it can't be felt), begin rubbing very lightly in a circular manner, at the rate of about one revolution per second. The pressure you apply should begin with about the same degree of pressure you would use to write your name on a steam-fogged mirror. You can use one finger, or two, whichever feels most comfortable to you and best matches the size of your partner.

Step 8
Stimulating the G-Spot

Okay, you're finally there, rubbing the G-Spot. . .so why isn't anything happening?

When you first touch the G-Spot, don't be surprised if you don't get an immediate reaction, just continue rubbing between the bottom of the valley and the back edge of the "textured" area.

In most cases, women will make comments such as "that feels good" or "stay right there" or "that feels so different". But if you don't get any response at all, don't panic. Think of the G-Spot as being similar to the nipple. When you first touch a nipple it is soft and only relatively sensitive. But as blood flows to the area and the nipple grows erect and aroused, the sensitivity increases in a dramatic flourish. The G-Spot is much the same. As you begin to caress it in a slow, circular manner, you will soon feel the area swell. It may become more porous and have an almost grainy feel. And it will most definitely become very sensitive.

If the G-Spot is massaged without prior arousal, many women find it uncomfortable. This is one of the key reasons that some people fail to find the G-Spot. Half-hearted pioneers often search for a spot that gives a woman great pleasure. Yet if these seekers blindly happen upon the G-Spot (without proper arousal) the woman may report minor discomfort or an "uncomfortable feeling", steering them away. This is an important point to remember in the future. If you try to move through the G-Spot technique faster in the future and skip over steps, the G-Spot may not be properly aroused when you reach it. Always follow the steps and watch for the "go ahead" signs from your partner as you move from one step to the next.

Rhythm is the absolute key here. As long as you maintain a steady rhythm, slow-building "waves" of ecstasy begin to wash in. Each wave that comes will be a little higher in intensity than the previous, and they will begin to cascade and surge faster and faster, until a point is reached that, just as one wave is beginning to fade, the next is already swelling.

If a women tries to stimulate her own G-Spot, her proclivity is often to stroke the area faster and firmer (and faster yet) as the waves grow more intense, trying to "*force*" a wave to crest and break over into the undying ecstasy she senses just beyond. The problem is, she can over-stimulate the G-Spot and inhibit the orgasm. This is critical knowledge to consider when you hear your lover's pleas to move faster or firmer. Be cautious about giving in. Maintain a slow even rhythm at first.

On the other hand, if you've been stimulating her G-Spot for ten minutes (or longer) at the one-revolution-per-second technique and she can't "crest over", it may be time to try a different touch. Remember that all women are different. Some women do need a slightly firmer touch. For others, a side-to-side or up-and-down finger movement is more effective than a circular one. Some women prefer stimulation with one finger while others prefer two or more. For yet others, slight variations in the speed are more effective. . . or a combination of any of these factors. This is where practice, judgment, and experimentation will come into play. We first recommend using the circular, light, one-revolution-per-second method. Our research has shown that it is the most effective. When many lovers were urged to move faster or firmer and the demand was obliged, the orgasm often faded instead of growing. When the original slow and light touch was resumed, success soon followed.

The good news is, there appears to be a "point of no return" with G-Spot orgasms. After her first experience, your lover will likely (ardently) convey this to you. Once she reaches the point where "waves" of pleasure are building and cascading rapidly, the orgasm becomes nearly inevitable.

We asked one woman if she could stop a clitoral or vaginal orgasm from occurring. She replied: "*Why, yes. Certainly.*" In discussing her G-Spot experience, the same woman stated: "*I reached a point where I couldn't stop it from coming, even if I wanted to!"*

When you finally get to witness the extreme ecstasy of your lover thrashing and screaming in the throes of pure ecstasy, it's very difficult not to become excited yourself and begin rubbing at the G-Spot with great enthusiasm. When some lovers see their partner in such ecstasy—especially if she has her first (visible) ejaculation—they often experience orgasm themselves. However, if you can maintain control and keep up the G-Spot stimulation, her orgasm may continue perpetually. This is how some couples state they can maintain an orgasm for up to 20 or more minutes! One couple even reported an orgasm that lasted 40 minutes and only stopped because neither partner could stand any more.

Step 9
The "Big-O" Draws Near

Even if your partner hasn't mentioned it yet, at this point she is likely aware that something quite different from a vaginal/clitoral orgasm is beginning to grow inside her. She may even feel some apprehension because of not knowing what's happening. So as you continue to stroke the G-Spot, be sure to reassure her that you are there, with her, in support of her, and remind her that you love her. Tell her of how beautiful she is and how much you enjoy taking this time to bring her pleasure. Not only will this make her feel emotionally safe and secure and help her climax sooner, it will also help her relax and lessen any guilt she may feel because of all the unselfish time you're spending. If she complains about feeling guilty, tell her you'll gladly let her return the favor another time, but tonight belongs to her.

In most cases, aside from the initial, slight swelling of the G-Spot, you won't notice any changes inside the vagina. When dealing with women who are new to the G-Spot orgasm, you'll often find the muscles in your forearm begin to burn before you feel the first vaginal contraction squeezing against your finger. Most of our survey respondents state "20 minutes" of G-Spot stimulation was required the first time. So again, it's time to utilize that patience and self-control. You haven't come this far to stop now. And if you do stop now, you'll likely disappoint your lover (who is aware of this massive ecstasy burgeoning inside her).

As the G-Spot orgasm grows near—The Big-O—the first thing you'll notice is a constricting of the vagina that begins with one of her "waves". With the next wave the vagina will constrict again, fade, then quickly return with the next wave, building and building to a point where the vagina is so perpetually constricted the muscles often spasm and quiver. Sometimes, the constricting is so tight it will eject your finger! About the same time you notice the first constriction, you'll also likely notice a greater sense of wetness. In fact, some women become *very* wet, to the point the suction of the finger causes slurping noises and a clear fluid actually begins to weep from the vagina. As we discussed earlier, this is the wonder of female ejaculation.

If this occurs, you may notice the consistency of this fluid differs from the normal milky lubricant produced by the vagina. Your finger may loose it's slickness, and since the area is so sensitive, you may want to pause and quickly apply an approved sexual lubricant. Have some lubricant available before things get started. As a general rule, the slicker your finger stays, the better.

Step 10
You're There!

You're there! As the wetness increases, the vagina will begin to convulse violently. As we mentioned, some women constrict so hard it forces the finger out of the vagina! By this time your lover will undoubtedly be thrashing wildly and screaming "Don't Stop! Don't Stop! Oh, God don't Stop!" or "Faster! Faster! Faster!" But regardless of how frantic your lover becomes, regardless of how excited you get by watching her ecstasy, try to control your motions.

As she finally crests over the top, most women will scream. It differs from the normal orgasm scream, being more of a guttural "expelling" sound rather than the gasping breaths of standard orgasms. If you can picture the grunting scream of a woman giving birth, her head hunched forward, clenching her knees, you're on the right track. . . and at the same moment she cries out, if she hasn't already done so she may ejaculate. This is especially true of G-Spot virgins. While it defies the findings of scientific research, many of our respondents mention the first G-Spot orgasm as the "wettest"—almost as if the fluid has been locked up for years and you're opening the dam, setting it free.

Our theory is that many of these couples simply don't "work" as hard on subsequent sessions as they did during the first G-Spot experience. Emotional bonding or the duration of stimulation may also play roles in determining the volume of fluid produced and the intensity of the orgasm. While these subjects are worthy of future exploration, they need not detain us here.

At this point, simply keep your finger moving until your lover asks you to stop or the orgasm fades. Typically, she will ride that wave for one or two full minutes, and the orgasm will lessen.

When you see this event, you will be completely rewarded for all your "work". Just watching her writhe and knowing the intense pleasure you are helping to provide is a great reward in itself.

Most men will want to join her as they sense this wave fading. The change from a finger to a swollen penis may delight her. . . and by this point, having watched her thrash and scream, feeling the warm wetness on your finger and hand, your self-control will likely be gone. So as long as she's willing, jump in and enjoy the orgasm with her. Feeling a wet, contracting vagina sucking at the penis can be an experience neither of you forget!

Afterwards

The Little Death

Directly after the orgasm, a few women pass through a phase called "the little death". This phase is a 5 to 10 second period in which the woman may appear to faint and/or seems to stop breathing. If this occurs, don't panic. Women who have passed through "the little death" frequently state they were so over-whelmed with pleasure they "floated in delirium" for a brief period. Other women may have a tendency to "pant" briefly before or during the orgasm, resulting in either hyperventilation or hypoventilation. In either case, a combination of the tremendous release of stress, sudden slowing of the heart, and a re-direction of oxygen-rich (or suddenly depleted) blood cells can bring about "the little death".

After 5 or 10 seconds, your lover should dreamily open her eyes. When you ask if she's okay—and you should—she'll likely tell you everything is fine, that she was simply enjoying the moment.

If your partner does actually faint and remains unresponsive for more than 15 or 20 seconds, you may have a medical emergency on your hands and should contact medical assistance immediately. Again, as a responsible party, it is your duty to know your partner's health status before engaging in sexual activity.

Sharing the Experience

In one survey, we asked women to express how they felt after their G-Spot experience. Women responding to this survey were instructed to indicate such by either "writing in" a comment or by choosing among (one or more) multiple-choice selections.

Of these respondents, an overwhelming 97% indicated feeling "Joyous/Elated" after their first G-Spot experience. Other leading answers were: "Lovey/Romantic"(89%), "Thankful" (84%), and "Satiated/Fulfilled" (82%).

While the vast majority of responses and comments were very favorable, an average of 47% also indicated feeling "embarrassment" and/or "curiosity" intermixed with other feelings. A few (3%), cited their feelings of embarrassment stemmed from becoming too "verbal" or "expressive" during the sexual episode. Yet a much larger group stated the embarrassment arose from fear they had "wet the bed" or "lost bladder control" during orgasm.

In some of these cases, women stated they had no idea females could ejaculate and therefore concluded they had "wet the bed". In other cases, women indicated awareness that "other" women could ejaculate, but previously considered themselves "non-ejaculators".

One tell-tale comment we frequently received was:

"I knew other women could ejaculate, but I didn't know I could."

As conscientious partners, it's important to be aware of this information. If your lover ejaculates during G-Spot stimulation, she may fear she has "wet the bed" and may hide or avoid discussing her "problem" due to personal embarrassment. Undoubtedly, she will feel bad about herself and equally bad about what's happened, even if the experience brought her great pleasure.

To thwart any hidden tensions from festering and rearing their heads in the future, be sure to talk openly with your partner about your first mutual G-Spot adventure. Discuss the phenomenon of female ejaculation. Learn how she feels about it: what she knows, or doesn't know. Reassure her that female ejaculations are physiologically normal. Reaffirm that they are natural and shouldn't be a source of embarrassment. Be open and honest. If you enjoyed it, tell her so. If it excited you, tell her so. If you're ready to go again, tell her so. Promote sexual expression. Explore. Try new positions. Be creative. Make it fun and loving.

Above all, make it good for both of you.

Self-Application

In today's market, there are many available sex-toys designed to stimulate the G-Spot. Among these toys are vibrating eggs (that can be inserted into the vagina), weighted balls that are inserted and worn inside the vagina (during common or sexual activities), and curved vibrators specifically designed to reach the G-Spot.

However, women do not need toys to enjoy what the G-Spot can offer. Self-stimulation is possible after finding a position that comfortably allows access.

While a few women can manage to self-stimulate in a reclined or supine position, most will find a squatted or sitting (with knees apart) position more accommodating.

Why? The answer is simple. Though it may be more comfortable "lying down", reaching the G-Spot (while in this position) requires a very flexible wrist, long fingers, and a short vagina.

There is also a second benefit to the "squatted" or "sitting" position. Upon first-time stimulation of the G-Spot, some women feel a sudden sensation of needing to urinate (discussed later in the "Problem Shooting" section). This can occur even if the woman has recently emptied her bladder.

To assuage the worry of accidental urination, we recommend self-stimulating while either squatted in the bathtub or seated on the toilet. These positions allow G-Spot access without the fear of "accidents". In addition, lubrication can be freely used, again without the worry of creating a "mess".

When self-stimulating, take as much time as needed to heighten arousal levels. Whether it's reading a sexy story, fantasizing, playing with sex toys, or simply massaging the breasts and body, do whatever raises your arousal and makes you feel that "ache" or "emptiness" within your vagina.

Once the vaginal craving begins to mount, you may begin exploring for the magic spot described in the earlier steps. At first touch the G-Spot may produce only mild pleasure. This is normal. However, as you continue to massage the area it will begin to swell and become more prominent.

Some women report that pushing down on the pelvis, just above the pelvic bone, helps in locating the G-Spot. When you believe you've located your special spot, move slowly. Whether you're using one finger or two, we recommend moving your fingers in a slow, lazy circle, as if you were tracing the rim of a nickel. Experiment. Try a light pressure at first, then a firmer touch. Tease yourself as you go. Make it deliciously slow and torturous. And above all, don't overlook the pleasure you feel along the way by rushing to the destination. Make the journey along the G-Spot pathway erotic and pleasing.

Exploring Other Possibilities

Before we expound on this topic, take a moment and congratulate yourself again. Stemming from the newly acquired knowledge you've gained from your investment in this book, you'll find yourself constantly aware of the G-Spot during all phases of foreplay and lovemaking. And because of this awareness, you and your partner will quickly learn to adjust and angle yourselves to promote G-Spot stimulation and derive greater pleasure during normal intercourse—something you would have never imagined prior to reading this book.

"How can a man derive more pleasure due to the G-Spot?" one might ask.

If you're male and you've seen a G-Spot orgasm, the answer to this question is blatantly obvious. For most males, the thought of having the penis inside a wet, spasming, tightly contracting vagina during G-Spot orgasm has unlimited appeal. And as you and your partner grow more familiar with the G-Spot, you may soon be able to cultivate G-Spot orgasms using the penis.

As an added benefit, as your partner grows more familiar and comfortable with G-Spot orgasms, she'll be able to attain them with greater speed, more reliability, and in a variety of coital positions, thus including the G-Spot in other realms of lovemaking, forging ahead toward blended orgasms.

"So where should we start?" you might ask.

As we mentioned in a previous section, there are a variety of sex toys available for stimulating the G-Spot. Most of these can be used by couples, as well as by oneself. Beyond the joys these toys offer, couples can also experiment with G-Spot-friendly coital positions.

"What are G-Spot-friendly coital positions?"

These are sexual positions that promote contact between the G-Spot and the penis. While there are a variety of G-Spot-friendly positions, the favored position is commonly referred to as "woman on top" position. In this position, the male lies on his back with legs slightly parted and extended flat. The female then straddles him, facing forward. This position is favorable because it is "face-to-face" and allows expression, kissing, nuzzling, and stimulation of the breasts during intercourse. It also allows the woman to angle her hips so the penis contacts her G-Spot. By leaning forward or backward, the woman can adjust the pressure of the penis against the G-Spot.

A second G-Spot-friendly position is a variation of the "missionary position". By placing a thick pillow (or two pillows) beneath the buttocks of the female (so she's lying with head down-hill), the penis will contact the G-Spot during entry.

G-Spot/penis contact also occurs (in the missionary position) when the male kneels of sits on folded knees, with his body upright of nearly upright. Or if the female places her calves or ankles on the male's shoulders as he enters her.

Another position is "doggy-style". If the male stands and the female bends at the waist at a partial angle (such as leaning forward with the hands braced against a wall) the underside of the penis will contact the G-Spot. For couples who are near the same height and enjoy sex in the shower, this is a very friendly position. However, the angle depends greatly on the male's penis. While some penises stand straight out during erection (at a 90 degree angle to the body), others tend to stand more upright with the penis head near the abdomen. In the case of the latter, the woman must stand nearly erect (or the man must lean forward) for G-Spot contact to be made.

Beyond these, there are numerous other positions that are G-Spot friendly. One couple reported their favorite position is with the woman sitting atop the washing machine, while the man stands facing her. They stated that during the spin cycle, the machine caused her G-Spot and vagina to vibrate against his penis, bringing both of them great pleasure and multiple climaxes. They also stated that if she faced the washer and leaned forward, the machine would vibrate against her clitoris while he entered her from behind.

Another couple stated they enjoy using a thin G-Spot vibrator with ample lubrication. As the woman neared climax, she would withdraw the vibrator and move it to her clitoris as her spouse entered her, allowing them to climax together.

Endless possibilities abound as you and your partner explore. And as you sample each pleasure, remember to also savor what you feel along the way. Take time and make it fun. Enjoy what the G-Spot can offer both of you.

Problem Shooting
Pain or Discomfort

If at any point your lover expresses pain while stimulating her vagina or G-Spot, stop the stimulation and schedule an appointment with her gynecologist. Although the G-Spot can cause very slight discomfort if massaged when not aroused, it should not cause true pain.

If she expresses feeling minor discomfort, try applying an approved sexual lubricant to prevent irritating the G-Spot's surface. Be sure you're not rubbing the surface to vigorously. Also, be sure your fingernails are smooth and cut short.

If she still feels pain or discomfort, she may suffer from a medical condition such as endometriosis, pelvic inflammatory disease, or a host of other potential causes. So a check-up with the gynecologist is in order.

Inability to Reach Orgasm

In rare cases, women simply can't attain the G-Spot orgasm. They'll reach a point were they are close, where the "waves" are building and fading and building and fading, but they simply can't crest over. This may be a physical problem but is most likely psychological. If this happens with your lover, the first step is to reassure her that you're there. Make emotional bonding your number one priority.

Second, if you haven't done so already, pause long enough to lubricate your hand and her vagina. Having ample lubrication can make an incredible difference.

Third, if you're absolutely sure she can't achieve the G-Spot orgasm, even with extra lubrication, break the "hand-above-breast" rule and try massaging the clitoris while you stroke her G-Spot. Be patient and understanding. And if your attempt for a G-Spot orgasm fails, you may wish to help her achieve a traditional clitoral or vaginal orgasm. Retry the G-Spot orgasm on another occasion. Afterwards, read the section titled "Emotional Aspects" and then re-read the 10 steps to make sure you're following the instructions to the letter. You may even want to discuss G-Spot orgasms with your lover. Some women simply won't allow themselves to "lose control" without understanding what's happening to their bodies.

Above all else, remember that orgasms are emotionally driven for most women. Talking, kissing, holding, reassuring, and building trust are each as important (sometimes more) than the physical stimulus.

The Urge to Urinate

Upon initial stimulation of the G-Spot, some women feel a strong and urgent need to urinate. This can be either a legitimate need or a "ghost sensation", depending on whether her bladder is full, partially full, or empty.

In the case of a full or partially full bladder, the pressure being applied near the urethra and bladder neck can bring about a real need to urinate. However, if the bladder was emptied recently, the sensation may originate from G-Spot stimulation.

Many women report feeling the "ghost sensation" upon the first few incidences of G-Spot stimulation. If ignored, the sensation usually abates and is replaced with erotic sensations. As a general rule, with repeated exposure and remembering to empty the bladder before intercourse, most women learn to get beyond this unpleasant sensation.

If your lover can't escape feeling "ghost sensations" after several attempts of G-Spot stimulation, a visit to her physician or gynecologist may be in order.

Orgasm Anxiety

Some couples set themselves up for failure through a condition we've dubbed "Orgasm Anxiety" (OA). This condition occurs when a person tries to "force" or "rush" an orgasm and inadvertently inhibits the orgasm from occurring. OA frequently occurs in people displaying certain behavior patterns: "Goal Seekers" and "Performance Givers" are the two most common.

Our definition of a "Goal Seeker" is a person who focuses strictly on achieving orgasm, placing little emphasis on the pleasure to be experienced along the way. "Goal Seekers" often express feelings of sexual frustration if they don't climax during each sexual encounter. Feelings of guilt, inadequacy, or selfishness may arise if they need additional stimulation after the partner has already climaxed—and any of these feelings can inhibit orgasm, thus perpetuating the problem. Goal Seekers who race their partner to orgasm and either "rush" or "try to force" the orgasm, suffer from OA.

Opposite to "Goal Seekers" are the "Performance Givers". PGs are known for "faking orgasms". While some people do not feel the need to climax for their own satisfaction, they may feel the need to orgasm to please their partner. It may be their partner feels inadequate if the "Performance Giver" doesn't climax; therefore, a "Performance Giver" can develop OA even though they don't require orgasm for their own benefit.

OA is a good subject to discuss candidly with your partner. Don't let "Goal Seeking" or "Performance Giving" steal your sexual enjoyment. Talk to your partner about *each* of you *enjoying more pleasure along the path of lovemaking*. Since it's very unlikely that you'll both achieve orgasm at the exact same moment, every time you make love, discuss your feelings of needing or giving stimulation after the other has climaxed. Discuss the importance you each place on climax. You may be surprised by what you learn.

He Said / She Said

One common problem between couples is a misinterpretation of "Foreplay". This misinterpretation comes about because men often think in physical terms while women often think in emotional terms. For many men, "foreplay" marks the physical acts which preface intercourse: kissing, touching, massage, fondling the breasts, vaginal or clitoral stimulation, cunnilingus, etc. . . These acts physically "ready" a woman for the "main event": intercourse and orgasm.

For many women, "foreplay" is primarily emotional with the physical stimuli being secondary. Women often view foreplay in wide and encompassing terms. Foreplay may range from spending an evening together, to talking, to sharing hopes and desires, slow dancing, or simply holding hands while walking through the mall or watching TV. At some undetermined point, foreplay becomes "Lovemaking".

Consider this example:

Wife: *"I'm almost afraid to kiss him. It's like one kiss leads us right to the bedroom. . ."*

Husband: *"She always complains that I jump right into it, but I don't. . . I kiss her, play with her breasts, massage her womanhood, and give her plenty of foreplay before we ever start. . ."*

This example clearly demonstrates the different perceptions. The "wife" feels there is no foreplay or intimacy because there was no emotional bonding prior to the physical. To her, the husband "jumps right into sex" because he starts at the point she perceives as the threshold of "lovemaking".

On the other hand, the husband is frustrated because he understands his wife's need for "foreplay" and feels he has tried to fulfill the need through physical stimulus (his concept of foreplay).

If any of this strikes home, be happy about it. Recognizing and accepting the problem is 95% of the way to resolve. What's important to realize is we can't glorify one of these needs while condemning the other. Neither can be deemed right or wrong. They are simply *differences*.

If you sense there may be confusion about foreplay in your relationship, have a candid chat with your partner about her needs. Be sure to share your needs with her, too. You may be surprised to learn how easily you can accommodate each other's needs while incidentally enriching and deepening your relationship. Even if you don't feel there's a problem in your relationship, it may help you to "shoot down" any troubles before they arise.

The Emotional Aspect

In the world of accounting, there's an adage that goes: "If you torture the numbers long enough, they'll tell you whatever you want to hear". "Truth" is much the same way. It can be distorted, twisted, omitted, hidden, or fashioned to whatever suits us best. If we manipulate the truth long enough, we'll eventually convince ourselves to believe whatever variation we've manufactured for the sake of our own emotional comfort. We can convert the *real* truth into a "falsehood". In straightforward terms, we often lie to ourselves and don't mind doing so if it shields us from the emotional pinpricks of life.

As we all know, the problem with self-deception is that the *real* truth has a nasty habit of haunting us. The truth doesn't care what we think of it. Unlike us, it has no ego to bruise. It is simply "the truth", like it or not.

Of women we've polled, the leading cause cited for the inability to obtain orgasm (of any type) was a lack of "emotional intimacy" being established. In another study, when women were asked: "What is it about sex that gives you the most pleasure?", the leading answer was "*emotional intimacy; sharing feelings with a loved one*". (This is especially true of Performance Givers; their motive for intercourse is emotional bonding.) Second and third rankings went to "*touching and sensuality*" and "*orgasm*". With such answers as "*pleasing him*", "*cunnilingus*", "*clitoral massage*", "*fellatio*", and "*the excitement*" ranking far near the bottom of the scale.

These two studies revealed two very simple truths: (1) that the lack of needed emotional intimacy can prevent many women from climaxing, and (2) that emotional intimacy is the engine driving most women's desire for intercourse.

If your lover was unable to reach a G-Spot orgasm, the most likely reason is she didn't reach a level of deep comfort. This is one of those nasty truths that most of us don't want to face, since it pains our ego. On the other hand, it's better to bear the pain and own up to the "possibility" and tackle it head-on, rather than lie to ourselves. . . only to have the ugly truth rear it's head again.

Whether your relationship is new or old, there is hope. The efforts you have put forth will not go unrewarded. If your relationship is new, it may be that she hasn't yet established a comfortable level of bonding with you. Perhaps she has reservations left over from a previous relationship. Be patient. Earn her trust. The positive factor is, you've lavished a wonderful evening on her that will certainly leave a favorable and romantic impression. She'll undoubtedly greet you with a wide smile the next time you meet.

If your relationship is more established, you may have overwhelmed your partner with an uncharacteristic amount of tenderness and bonding. She may have been expecting you to "drop a bomb" at any moment and simply couldn't completely relax. This is especially true if sex has recently been a ritual.

So what are you waiting for?

Talk to your partner. If you enjoyed the evening tell her so and ask how she enjoyed it. If you both agree that you mutually enjoyed it, this is the perfect opportunity to plan for the next time. Chances are, next time she'll be more relaxed and you'll succeed.

Tips From Experienced Users

While the 10-Step Technique has proven effective for most people, it's important to recall that we are each individuals. We each have different likes and dislikes. We each have distinct perceptions of life, personal experiences, our own spiritual views, and subtle idiosyncrasies that make us unique. Like snowflakes falling from a winter sky, we are the same when viewed collectively, yet individual when examined more closely. We are "who we are", and no one is exactly the same as any of us.

Because of this, we encourage you to adapt the 10-Step Technique to best serve the needs of you and your partner. Carve your own niche. Be creative and adventurous. Make it upbeat and fun. Be romantic and spontaneous. But above all, be the person your partner fell in love with. Be the unique person you are.

Below are comments and tips shared by users of the 10-Step Technique. In some cases, these individuals blazed their own pathways to G-Spot adventure. Adapt what you can and enhance your own G-Spot experience:

"My wife and I both work corporate jobs. After working 10 hours a day, fighting traffic during frantic commutes to and from work, then getting through supper, housework, yard work, and putting up with the day-to-day headaches of life, my wife and I are exhausted by late evening. By 8:00 PM, we're both ready to sit back, relax, and unwind, then go to bed so we can do the whole thing over again the next day. Often, we're too tired to even make love.

Because of this, on our 'date night' I surprised my wife with a special treat. On Friday morning, I sent her flowers at work with a note to expect a 'very special and romantic' evening at home. I took the afternoon off, cleaned the house, made some prepara-tions, and had a candlelight dinner waiting when she walked in from work. After the dinner, I prepared a hot bath and loaded the bathroom with scented candles. While she soaked and relaxed in the tub, I cleaned the kitchen, put on soft music in the bedroom, lit more candles there, and sprinkled the bed with rose petals. When she finished her bath, I led her to the bedroom and gave her a full-body massage with her favorite aromatherapy oils. I started with her back, then the backs of her legs, then her feet. I spent an hour or more just massaging and teasing her. It was a great turn-on for both of us. By the time I finished the massage, she was relaxed and in a casual state. The atmosphere was romantic, and we were both aroused and in a sexually comfortable state. It was the perfect lead-in to the latter steps of your technique. From there, everything happened naturally." - J.P.

"My girlfriend and I use the flavored body lotions you can buy through adult catalogs. We like the types that feel hot when you lick or blow them. She loves it when I tie her down, blind-fold her, and then spread the lotion on her breasts and all over her vagina. It drives her crazy when I suck her breasts and rub the lotion on her clitoris and G-Spot. Sometimes I even alternate between the lotion and an ice cube to really make her scream." - W.R.

"The key to success is the presence of romance. It's much easier to orgasm when you're feeling loved and connected with your partner." - A. P.

"Sometimes the muscles in my forearm cramp-up while I'm rubbing her G-Spot. I've found that keeping a G-Spot vibrator next to the bed is a good idea in case my hand cramps. The secret is to buy a thin one. Some of the vibrators available are so big that when she starts contracting they become uncomfortable." - K. R.

"The great thing about the G-Spot is you can do it nearly anywhere. On our first 'date night', I was really eager and started fingering my wife and massaging her G-Spot during the movie.

She was moaning quietly and orgasmed within five minutes. It was exciting for both of us because we were doing it in public." - Anonymous

"My wife and I like to lie on our sides in a 69 position. I can perform cunnilingus and massage her G-Spot while she gives me head or massages me with lotion. It drives us both crazy." - R. G.

"Before we learned your technique, I had seriously considered having my breasts augmented because my husband tended to ignore them. I think that reading your book helped him grasp the importance of kissing and fondling my breasts. Whether a woman's breasts are small or large, it's usually very pleasurable having them nuzzled and played with. I know several women who feel this way. Stimulating the breasts is an important part of love-making for me. Thanks for emphasizing this in your book." - C. S.

"It's critical that foreplay start long before you reach the bed-room." - Anonymous

"At first, my wife had a lot of trouble with the false sensation of needing to urinate when she neared orgasm. We got beyond this by doing it in the shower." - C. H.

"If you want a thrill, have her lie on her back. Lie on your side facing her. Have her throw her nearest leg over top your legs so you can rub her G-Spot and slide your [penis] inside her at the same time. That way, your finger is massaging her G-Spot and your [penis]! When she starts contracting, it will drive you both crazy." - D. J.

"Keep a fresh towel and lots of lubrication in the bedroom." - D. T.

"The clitoris can really distract a women. Stay away from it the first few times you use the technique. You'll have time for it later." - R.B.

"For a real treat, try having her lie on her back on a table or counter. Have her bottom positioned near the edge. If you squat in front of her, you can hold her labia open and watch as she orgasms and ejaculates. It's amazing to see the juice flow down your hand as her vagina contracts and sucks on your finger." - T. W.

"I had a lot of misconceptions before I read this book. I thought I could always hit a women's G-Spot with my penis. Although it stings the ego, it's better to realize you were wrong than continue being wrong." - L. J. T.

"My wife uses a vibrator on her clitoris while I massage her G-Spot and suck her breasts. Her orgasm is strong enough she sometimes faints afterwards. She loves it." - T. P.

"I love seeing my wife in a teddy, a garter, thigh highs, and high heels. I'm a leg and breast man and that ensemble is a real turn-on for me. However, before I learned your technique, I had to beg my wife to dress up for me in her 'play clothes'. Now she meets me at the door in her 'play clothes' every day after work. Thank you." - D. L.

"The first time she came, it looked like she was about to give birth. She hunched forward and all this fluid shot out of her and splattered on my arm. I didn't believe in the G-Spot until that moment. Believe me, it's real." - T. J. S.

"If you don't succeed the first try, don't give up. It's worth it when it finally happens. And it will eventually happen when she's ready." - F. S.

An Informative Interview
with a
Renowned Sex Researcher

A note from the author regarding this interview:

According to *The Merriam-Webster Dictionary* (Pocket Books), the word "philanthropy" is defined as:

"an effort to promote human welfare; a charitable act or gift; (or) goodwill to fellowmen...".

When delving deeper into philanthropy's meaning, a synonym encountered is "altruism", which is defined as:

"an unselfish act performed for the welfare of others".

While "philanthropy" and "altruism" are very similar in meaning, a subtle difference does exist in their meanings and usage. "Philanthropy" places emphasis on the "act" of helping others. In other words, when we donate our time or money to a charitable organization, we are performing acts of "philanthropy". Being a philanthropist can make us feel better about ourselves and may provide either public recognition or a nice break on our yearly taxes, possibly both.

Like philanthropy, "altruism" also entails a donation of our time or money in a manner that benefits a group, community, or humankind in general. However, altruism takes the concept of philanthropy to a higher level because it is performed *without any desire for self-recognition.* Altruism is very unselfish. Anonymous donations are altruistic acts, and in our present day "me-me" world, such acts are rare, commendable, and morally refreshing.

I have touched upon "philanthropy" and "altruism" because the interview subject for this section displays both of these admirable traits and characteristics. While wishing to remain "anonymous", he or she unselfishly donated their own time and effort...purely for the sake of insuring that you, the reader, received accurate information. And because of my profound respect for "Anonymous", even though I wish to share recognition, I have sworn to protect his or her identity. I can only say that "Anonymous" is a world-renowned leader in the fields of sexology and sexual research. And that disclosing his or her identity would add instant creditability to this book. He or she is widely considered an expert in this field, if not *"the"* expert of the field, and I would urge readers to regard his or her interview answers as reliable and well informed.

The Interview:

AUTHOR: I'd like to begin the interview by thanking you on behalf of myself and readers for sharing your time and your wealth of knowledge. Your unselfish generosity is commendable.

ANONYMOUS: You're welcome.

AUTHOR: The first question I wish to pose is a preface to the overall G-Spot experience: what elements do you feel are important for a woman to achieve a G-Spot orgasm?

ANONYMOUS: A woman has to be comfortable with her body, comfortable and willing to communicate with her partner, and has to be willing to experiment with different positions of sexual intercourse. Acceptance of self is very important. A woman also has to be aware that she is responsible for her own orgasm, and no one can give her an orgasm.

AUTHOR: If we can, let's break that down a little more by examining an "orgasm". Exactly what is an orgasm?

ANONYMOUS: It's important to distinguish that in men, orgasm and ejaculation are two different phenomenon and are controlled by two separate nerve pathways. We are just beginning to learn more about the neurophysiology of sexual response and sexual behavior in women. As individuals, we say we know what an orgasm is, but I'm not sure we know what it is. In layman's terms, there's a stimulation of nerve pathways, a buildup of tension, and then a release of muscle tension. And you do not have to have physical stimulation for orgasm to occur. This can also occur with mental stimulation.

AUTHOR: With that in mind, how do G-Spot orgasms differ from clitoral or vaginal orgasms?

ANONYMOUS: There are physiological differences in that with stimulation of the G-Spot, the uterus pushes down into the vagina, the introitis of the vagina opens and there is a bearing down sensation. With stimulation of the clitoris, the uterus pulls up, the end of the vagina balloons out, and there are contractions in the outer third of the vagina. Women report that an orgasm from G-Spot stimulation feels deeper inside, whereas an orgasm from clitoral stimulation is more localized in the genital area.

AUTHOR: Do you feel that female ejaculations and the G-Spot coincide?

ANONYMOUS: Not necessarily. In some women they are correlated, in others they are not. In one of the early research articles published on this, research showed a test subject had ejaculation from clitoral stimulation and from G-Spot stimulation.

AUTHOR: Do all women ejaculate?

ANONYMOUS: Most women do have some expulsion of fluid from the ducts and glands into the urethra. And this can occur during clitoral stimulation or vaginal stimulation or G-Spot stimulation. The fluid goes either into the bladder or out of the urethra as ejaculation. This has been documented by Dr. Francesco Cabello of Malaga, Spain.

AUTHOR: What is known of the fluid women expel during an ejaculation — where is it stored, what is it's chemical makeup or nearness?

ANONYMOUS: It comes from the female prostate gland, which surrounds the urethra and has ducts into the urethra. It is made up of glucose, fructose, PSA, and PAP.

AUTHOR: What health benefits or risks surround G-Spot orgasms?

ANONYMOUS: The obvious benefit is it feels good. Risks could be that someone trying to find it could cause trauma to tissue with long finger nails or improper stimulation or not getting feed-back from the woman. Also, stimulation of this area produces a strong natural pain blocking effect.

AUTHOR: About how far inside the vagina is the G-Spot?

ANONYMOUS: The G-Spot is found about half-way between the back of the pubic bone (which is on the roof of the vagina) and the cervix, and it's along the course of the urethra. You have to push into the upper vaginal wall to feel this area as it swells. Use a "come here" motion with your fingers to stimulate the area.

It's really hard for women to feel it on themselves unless they have a short vagina and long fingers, because you have to bend down, push up, and push in... although there are instructions on how to find it on yourself. It is difficult to say how far inside the vagina you have to feel because the G Spot is felt through the upper vaginal wall, not on it, and each woman is different.

AUTHOR: What would you tell people about finding the G-Spot?

ANONYMOUS: I don't want to see people set up on finding the G-Spot, or male multiple orgasms, or female ejaculation, or imagery orgasm as a goal they have to achieve. We're all unique individuals. We all have different tastes in terms of the clothing we choose to wear, the foods we choose to eat, the people we choose to be with. I think it's only natural that we have different tastes in what we like sexually. And some women may not find this area sensitive or erotic. Or it may be that someone is not pressing hard enough on the area, because you have to use quite a bit of pressure pushing up through the vaginal wall to feel the area swell. Or they may have long fingernails or rough skin that causes the women to feel uncomfortable.

What's important is we need to be open and aware and help people find whatever is pleasurable for them, whether that be G-Spot stimulation, clitoral stimulation, or stimulation of other erotic areas. And more importantly, we should enjoy the overall experience and what's felt along the way, not just focusing on achieving an orgasm.

What we need to do is enjoy the experience, not just strive for an orgasm.

AUTHOR: What would help women to learn more about themselves?

ANONYMOUS: Men are given permission to touch their penis when they urinate. But for women it's more difficult. Many women get the message as a young child: "don't touch down there". And it's very difficult for these women to learn about their own bodies because they have been given negative messages about touching their genitals. And you can't learn about yourself without exploring and touching your genitals and without touching other parts of your body. So women need to learn to be comfortable touching their body for pleasure.

AUTHOR: What will happen if all women become orgasmic?

ANONYMOUS: There's so much more to sensuality and sexuality than orgasm. And women are often orgasmic now. But that's not the end-all. That is not it. It's the relationship, the communication, the caring, and the intimacy that are so important. And don't be threatened by a woman's sexuality and sensuality, she's going to enjoy it and you enjoy her enjoying it.

AUTHOR: What can people do to increase their sexual response?

ANONYMOUS: I think it's important for women to be aware that they can take control and do some things that will help themselves...not only in terms of mapping their bodies and being aware of what provides them with pleasure. They can use the Kegel exercises. The Kegel exercises are those that are sometimes taught around the time of childbirth, before or after, to increase the strength of the PC muscle. By increasing the strength of this muscle, we find that there is a positive correlation with how strong that muscle is and a women's orgasmic response. That is, women who have very weak muscles usually don't have orgasms, where women who have particularly strong muscles often have multiple orgasms. This was documented by Graber and Klein-Graber in the 1970's.

To identify the muscle to use with the Kegel exercises, become aware of the muscle you use to cut off the flow of urine. You may want to test the strength of your Pubococcygeus or PC muscle before you start the exercise program. Put two fingers into the vagina, yours or your partners, open them up like scissors, and then try to close them with your muscles. Don't be surprised if you can not do that.

Start off the exercises slowly, contracting and relaxing the muscles you use to cut off the flow of urination, slowly building up the repetitions to 100 times per day. Then in a month, repeat the test by inserting two fingers into the vagina and trying to squeeze the fingers together to see if the muscle is getting stronger. This is a good way for women to take control of their health and their sexual response.

Not only is it good for women to do, they are also good for men. Men can do the same exercise to increase sexual pleasure and orgasm. Men have reported that their erections are stronger after strengthening the PC muscle. By increasing the strength of this muscle and then squeezing the muscle at the moment of ejaculatory inevitability, some men can learn to have multiple orgasms through preventing ejaculation. Here again, it's important to realize that ejaculation and orgasm are two separate phenomenons and need not occur simultaneously.

AUTHOR: If a woman does Kegel exercises, will her vagina be tighter?

ANONYMOUS: It may become tighter. As the strength of the PC muscle increases she may feel tighter during vaginal intercourse. And also, a very good way of doing the exercise is with a penis inside the vagina. You're then doing the exercises against a resistance device, which is always more effective. And also, the male will have pleasure and enjoyment from the stimulation of the penis by the PC muscle.

AUTHOR: How can a man test the strength of their PC muscle?

ANONYMOUS: There's a very fun way for men to test the strength of their PC muscles. First of all, you want to do this in private. When you start out, before you do the exercise, put a tissue over an erect penis and lift it up. And most men will smile and say "I can do that", but that's a pretty weak muscle. So after they do the exercise for a month or so [the same as the women do by contracting then relaxing the muscle that stops the flow of urination], they can try the test again. Then, they may try doing the test with a wash cloth, and then a hand towel, and eventually a wet hand towel. But don't do the exercise with something over the penis. This is just to test the strength of the muscle. The exercise is for fun and sexual enjoyment.

AUTHOR: What affect does aging have on sexual response?

ANONYMOUS: There are some physiological changes during the aging process. Men and women may take a little longer as they get older to become sexually aroused. It may take longer for men to have an erection and may take longer for ejaculation. For women, it may take longer to have vaginal lubrication. Also, women may not have as many contractions as they once did, and the contractions may not be as strong. But instead of comparing the process to how it was, it is important to enjoy sensual and sexual as it is. Here again, the Kegel exercises can help in keeping sexuality more vital.

AUTHOR: In closing, I'd like to thank you once again for sharing your knowledge with readers. It is appreciated and I'm sure readers can benefit through the information you've provided.

Case Studies & Worksheets

Female Responses

Subject: A
      Female, age: 49
      Marital Status: Married/Divorced/Re-married

Subject: B
      Female, age: 32
      Marital Status: Married

Subject: C
      Female, age: 25
      Marital Status: Single, engaged

Prior to you (or your mate) having read this book, had you experienced a G-Spot orgasm?

A: No.

B: No.

C: I'd never felt anything like it. . .

Before your first G-Spot experience, did you climax on a regular basis through intercourse?

A: Yes and no. During my first marriage, I never climaxed and hated having sex. My ex-husband was rough, selfish, and impatient. Sex with him was painful and never a source of pleasure for me. It was the sore point of our marriage. He called me "frigid" and he didn't understand why I never enjoyed sex. He acted as if something was wrong with me, and after hearing it over and over, I began to believe him. I tried talking to my mother and grandmother about the problem, but found no support. They presented sex as the duty of a "good wife" in fulfilling her husband's needs and as a means of procreating.

The first time I made love with my present husband, it was a totally new experience. He's patient and gentle, and I climaxed several times the first night we made love. It was a true awakening and gave me a sense of renewed self-confidence. It made me realize that I wasn't "frigid"—there wasn't anything wrong with me—and I wasn't solely responsible for the first failed marriage. Now, I nearly always climax. When I feel my husband beginning to swell inside me, it throws me right over the edge. And on the rare occasions when he climaxes before I do, he helps me achieve by either continuing to move, oral stimulation, or with sexual props. We never have a problem because we talk openly and I don't end up feeling "rushed".

B: No. I can sometimes climax when my husband orally stimulates my clitoris or uses a vibrator, but can't [climax] with just his penis. I need lots of cuddling and loving beforehand to get me in a sensual mood.

C: Not every time. It depended on the guy. . . how I felt about him and my mood when it happened.

How much did you enjoy sex before your first G-Spot orgasm?

A: With my second husband, I've always enjoyed making love.

B: That's a hard question to answer. . . Our sex life was good, but nothing like it is now. I guess I felt that something was missing. . . like there should be deeper pleasure and intensity—do you understand what I mean?

("Yes. . .")

"I'd find myself reading romance novels and dreaming of someday feeling the kind of pleasure those women feel. But I wasn't sure if that was real or merely the yearnings of fiction.

C: Sometimes I enjoyed it; other times, if I really liked a certain guy, it was an easy way to deepen the relationship.

Can you describe the first time you experienced a G-Spot orgasm?

A: Yes. I'll never forget it. But where should I begin? Okay. Let's see. . . I'd have to say my husband blind-sided me with it. He never gave me a single clue that he'd read the book or what he was planning. He just asked me out on a "date"—and considering that we're married, I felt that his "asking me out" was flattering. It was a very romantic gesture and I was looking forward to making it up to him, come date night.

When our "date" finally rolled around, he surprised me by coming home from work with a dozen roses. We went out to dinner (which I loved because I didn't have to cook or do clean-up afterwards). Then after dinner, we went for a moonlight stroll, then came home and cuddled on the sofa while watching a movie.

I guess I was aroused because I had been looking forward to "making it up to him" all week. And he was aroused too, probably by his secret agenda. We ended up necking through most of the movie—just like we were teenagers—until we got home and I was so ready I stripped off my clothes and most of his. I wanted him then and there. . .

Instead, he picked me up and carried me to the bedroom, laid me on the bed, finished undressing, and began kissing me all over again.

In retrospect, having read the book now, I can see how he was following the steps. But he was also concentrating his attention on me, and I could feel it. His attention was focused much deeper than our regular love-making. We had a connection going. It was almost spiritual. And even though I was ready for him at any moment, I didn't feel rushed, and loved what he was doing to me.

He nuzzled and sucked my breasts until I felt like my whole body was yearning for him. And by the time he finally touched me, I thought I would explode. It was like tuning guitar strings, tweaking them tighter and tighter until you just know that the next turn of the knob they're going to go. I can remember pushing and thrusting against his hand, begging him to massage me, yet loving the way he was teasing me.

When he finally entered me with his finger and began massaging my G-Spot, the tension drained from me and I felt like I was floating in the clouds. It was relaxing to have that hungry void filled, while I was still highly aroused. I'm not really sure how to describe it. . . It's like hot and cold. He was sucking and teasing my breasts, which made me yearn. But his finger was fulfilling the void with every new yearning. It was heaven.

A few minutes into it, I could tell something totally new was happening inside me. I don't know how to describe it, but I could feel an orgasm building and knew it would be *much* deeper and *much* more intense than anything I'd ever felt before. There was a great sense of *building*. I can't put it into words. It was scary. I wanted it to happen yet I knew I'd have to let myself go completely to reach it. And that was hard to do. I didn't want to make a fool of myself in front of my husband, thrashing around or screaming. At the same time, I was afraid he'd stop what he was doing and I'd be terribly disappointed.

He must have felt me tense up or something at that very moment—maybe it was the connection we had. . . I don't know—but he said exactly what I needed to hear. He told me: *"Don't worry. I'm here. I know what's happening to you. I love you. Just relax and let it happen."*

And I did. I could feel it building inside of me, like waves, each a little higher than the last. He continued telling me how much he loved me and reassuring me. I'm not sure how he was able to talk because I never felt his mouth leave my breasts, but he did it somehow.

A couple of times I peaked out really high and was close to cresting over. I wanted it to happen *so badly*, yet was afraid it wouldn't, and part of me was a little wary of it. But after the third or fourth peak,—just when I started to think I wasn't going to make it—I felt this warmth start inside of me, spreading outward from my core. I could feel it building and building and building and I realized then, even if I wanted to stop it, I couldn't.

When it finally came I screamed and was squinting my eyes closed so hard that I could see red. I could feel myself contracting hard against his finger, trying to suck it in, getting warmer and tighter and warmer and tighter. . . It was by far the best thing I'd ever felt—better than I imagined. I don't really have words to describe it. It just felt so good and kept going and going much longer than any orgasm I'd ever had. It was so warm and so deep. . . I wanted it to last forever.

After what seemed like an eternity (which my husband later told me was two-and-a-half minutes), it began to fade. I became vaguely aware that the bed and the inside of my thighs were very wet. For a minute, I wondered if I had lost control and peed the bed during the climax. . . but I forgot about that as my husband quickly removed his finger and inserted himself inside of me. He was obviously highly aroused, was rock hard, and began swelling almost instantly. His penis felt about three times its normal size and he was marveling about how tight I was. He came right away and his swelling threw me right over the edge again and we climaxed together.

After we laid together panting for a few minutes and floated back down to earth, I realized that the bed actually was wet. Very wet. It was absolutely drenched. I felt certain I had lost control of myself and was very embarrassed. That first time was the wettest I've ever been. But he assured me I hadn't peed, that a stream of clear fluid had shot out of me and was gushing past his hand and splattering between my knees.

I would say I was skeptical, but skeptical may not be a precise description of what I felt. I think "wonderment" is a more appropriate term. I was astonished, stunned, and curious at the same time. I had to examine some of the fluid on my thighs just to reassure myself. It didn't smell like urine and was clear, with just a hint of milkiness. And it was slick—not as slick as my normal lubricant, but not nearly as sticky as urine.

Afterwards, he explained how he had come across the book and how it had piqued his curiosity. He showed me the book and we read parts of it and talked about how women have the ability to ejaculate (as I had).

I've got to admit, I loved him more right then than I ever remember loving anything. What he did for me—for us—was so selfless. And since then, our relationship has never been stronger.

B: Not in a single word. It was the best thing I've ever felt.

("Better than other orgasms you'd had?")

Oh, yes. . . by a long shot. In the past, when my husband made love to me, I'd get really keyed up about the time he was ready to go to sleep. The problem was, as soon as he came the "show was over". I don't want you to get the wrong idea here—I love my husband dearly and enjoy making love with him—but it was frustrating to watch him have such a fulfilling orgasm and then fade off to sleep while I was left tossing and turning and wanting more.

On some nights I'd feel satisfied. Other times, one or two orgasms just weren't enough for me. The problem wasn't the quantity of orgasms, it was the quality. The depth. The orgasms I had with my husband (and other men before my marriage) just weren't deep enough. They left me sensing there should be more, which ties in with what I mentioned earlier about the romance novels and wanting to feel the deep satisfaction those fictional women feel.

After that first G-Spot orgasm, I knew I'd found what I was missing. I felt completely satisfied afterwards. I was drained— (laugh)—literally.

C: Intense pleasure. That's the only way I know how to describe it. It was very different from anything I'd felt. As strange as it sounds, I'm glad it hadn't happened earlier in my life because I wouldn't have anything to compare it to.

After your first G-Spot experience, has it been easier or harder for you to achieve G-Spot orgasms? And how do they compare to the first experience?

A: The second time my husband tried the technique it took longer for me to climax. I had a really hard time reaching it and ended up "giving up" before it finally happened. I think my husband had relaxed a little and wasn't following all of the steps to the letter. . . and in some ways, that was a reversion back to our previous lovemaking. Not that it was bad before. . . I just wanted to feel his focus and the emotional bond we had the first time.

Part of the problem was my own, too. I wanted to feel the climax *so badly* that I tried to rush it. But I've since learned that this isn't something you can *make* happen. Every time I tried to force it to happen, it faded away just when I was ready to crest over. It reminded me of a wanderer in the desert chasing a mirage. You know? The faster you run after it, the farther away it gets.

After getting really-really close five or six times, I gave up. I began to cry because I was afraid that the first time had been a fluke and I'd never get to feel another climax like that first one again. Plus, my husband had been caressing the spot for about 45 minutes and I was feeling guilty and selfish. I knew he wanted to climax, too, and I figured his hand was getting tired and was probably hurting. It was frustrating and made me see the wisdom behind your advising people [in the book] not to tell the woman about it beforehand. Once you know how good it's going to be, the apprehension is almost painful and can be inhibiting."

("Did you eventually reach the climax?")

Yes. I told my husband that I couldn't make it and asked him to stop. By then, I'd given up completely. I was very disappointed. He stopped caressing my G-Spot and started caressing my breasts and abdomen while we talked. He told me that I was probably trying too hard and I just needed to try to relax and let it happen naturally. I remember telling him that I couldn't relax because I wanted it to happen too badly, but was afraid it would never happen again. I also told him I was feeling guilty for how long it was taking, and he told me not to feel guilty, that he enjoyed seeing me feel good. He told me that he loved me and asked me if massaging the G-Spot felt good even when I didn't completely make it. I told him yes, and I loved him, too. He asked if I would let him try again and would just relax and enjoy what I was feeling at the moment instead of focusing on the climax. By then, I was beginning to feel a vaginal yearning again and didn't need much convincing. He teased me a little more and then began caressing my G-Spot again. As soon as he touched it, I could feel another wave start building, but instead of trying to make it come, I tried to focus on what I was feeling. Within 30 seconds, I climaxed.

Since then, I've learned not to try to force it to happen. And the more we do it, the easier it is for me. We've done it standing in the shower, on the washing machine during the spin cycle, the couch; anyplace works fine.

B: I had a few slow times at first. I had to be lying down and had to make myself relax. But after the first few times it got faster and easier. And now I can ejaculate right away and can do it in other positions. Once we did it while standing in the shower. And sometimes now I have a G-Spot orgasm when I take the top during regular lovemaking. It's never been as good as the first time it happened, but it's come close and it's still more fulfilling than other orgasms. You won't hear me complaining.

C: It keeps getting better and better.

Male Responses

Subject: A
> Male, age: 38
> Marital Status: Married

Subject: B
> Male, age: 34
> Marital Status: Married

Subject: C
> Male, age: 27
> Marital Status: Single, engaged

Did you succeed on your first attempt to give a G-Spot orgasm?

A: Yes.

B: No.

C: Yes.

Approximately how long did it take from the beginning of the actual G-Spot stimulation until the orgasm began?

A: The first time took about 45 minutes. About 30 minutes into it, my forearm started burning and lightly cramping. It wasn't overly painful, but it was enough to cause doubts about the system and my wife's "supposed" ability to have a G-Spot orgasm. However, I could tell something was happening with my wife by the way she was moaning and moving and telling me not to stop. I figured if nothing else, it was a great workout for the muscles in my forearm and a thorough test for the system if I could keep it up a few more minutes. By the 40-minute mark, my arm felt like it was on fire and I was having trouble keeping my finger movement steady. This worked out for the best because, by then, my wife had started urging me to go faster. I could see the desperation in her eyes and I wanted to go faster—and would have if I could—but my forearm muscles wouldn't allow it. It was the agonizingly slow pace that pushed her right over the edge. Had I moved faster or harder, I would have delayed her climax without realizing it.

The second time took a while, too. But since then we've gotten faster and faster at bringing the climax about. Now, we can often do it within 5 minutes. We can use other positions and I can often insert myself just before it happens so we climax together.

B: 20 minutes.

C: 25-30 minutes.

Have you always succeeded?

A: About 99 percent of the time.

B: Ah. . . no. I'm embarrassed to mention this, but when I first got the book I didn't read it. I scanned through it, looked at the diagram, and tried stimulating my wife's G-Spot the next time we had sex. When I asked her how it was feeling she said it was "different" and "unusual" and "it felt good" but nothing seemed to be happening. She kept guiding my hand back to her clitoris, so I stopped and figured the whole thing was a hoax.

A few days later I got to work early and my boss called on the cell-phone and said he'd be running about half-an-hour late. It was about 20 degrees outside and since I didn't have a key to get inside, it meant I'd have to wait in the car until he got there. I have to wonder if there wasn't some divine intervention going on because I'd hidden the book under the car seat and had nothing better to do than read it. The funny thing is, I finished the last page just as my boss turned into the parking lot.

As I read the book, I realized the mistakes I'd made and figured it was worth another try, this time following the steps instead of trying to muddle my way through it.

It went like clockwork. Since then, my wife has G-Spot orgasms every time I use the technique and our relationship has never been stronger.

C: Most of the time. I think it depends on the girl.

What was the most extraordinary or remarkable thing you learned from this book?

A: I didn't know my wife had the ability to ejaculate before I read the book. I thought only a few women could "squirt" (as they call it) and guessed these women had some type of physical anomaly which allowed the squirting. It made them perfect candidates for porn movies.

Now I've learned the opposite is true of what I believed. From the book, I've learned that most women have this inherent capacity. And it's amazing that so many people are still unaware of it. Totally unbelievable.

B: Before I read the book, I thought the whole G-Spot thing was a hoax. I thought that my wife *did* ejaculate when she achieved orgasm and it was a small amount that mixed right in with her natural lubrication. I'm glad I was wrong! The first time she had a G-Spot orgasm she drenched the bed. We were in bed with the lights off, so I couldn't see the fluid coming out of her. But I could feel my hand and the bed getting soaked. And later, when we turned on the lights to change the sheets, there was about a foot-wide wet circle where she was lying. I was shocked that all the G-Spot stuff was true.

C: The whole thing, the strength of the orgasm and the ejaculation. The first time I did it, I was with an ex-girlfriend I'd been dating off-and-on for about 4 months. We'd had sex a few times and it was good, but not great. She was always quiet during sex and would just lie there motionless and moan a little bit. And then afterwards, she would act like I owed her some big favor. But that first night [using the G-Spot technique] was wild and different! At first she just started moaning like usual. But her moans kept getting louder and louder and she started saying "Oh, God, don't stop! Oh, God, don't stop!" over and over. Then she started bucking and gasping and kept getting louder and louder until she was screaming it. I was loving it! I half-expected the cops to show up at any minute because the walls in my apartment are paper-thin. But she didn't seem to care, she kept screaming. She looked like she was in labor and was giving birth. Then she went dead silent and was really straining and all this fluid started kind of bubbling and flowing out of her. It was awesome. She followed me around like a whipped puppy for a week afterwards and wanted to do it all day and night.

What do you enjoy most about G-Spot orgasms?

A: Wow. That's a tough question. There's more than one answer. For one thing, I like seeing the pleasure my wife is experiencing and knowing that *I* provided that pleasure for her. It's very satisfying and it lends a certain sense of both love and power. But it runs deeper than just that. Before I learned this technique, when my wife would climax I never had distinct physical signs to go by. She could have easily faked it and I'd have no way of knowing differently. I simply had to take her word for it. There were no distinct guideposts. When she neared a climax, her breathing would increase. I might feel a very slight tightening in her vagina and her moaning would grow louder, but that was it. There was never a clear beginning or end.

Now all the doubt is gone. I have undeniable physical signs to go by. As she starts the climax, her vagina begins constricting and squeezing against my finger so tightly that it threatens to force my finger out! She's so tight and wet and warm that it drives me crazy. And then the fluid comes and her moans turn to screams. There's simply no more doubt about when the climax begins and when it ends.

B: This technique has truly revitalized my marriage. My wife and I are closer and more open now than we've ever been before. Our sex life is great and our relationship is stronger than ever.

Our relationship changed drastically the first time she had the G-Spot orgasm. I think it comes down to trust. When it was happening, I realized that it was so extremely intense for her that she was putting all of her trust in me, completely. She had to let go fully and shed all inhibitions in order to reach it. By doing that, she was handing me the reigns of control. She was giving me all the power and trusting that I wouldn't abuse it or make fun of her afterwards or let harm come to her while it was happening. And that even though she wasn't sure what was physically happening to her, she trusted me to guide her through it.

When I realized just how much trust she was showing, it touched me deeply. All the barriers that life had silently erected between us crumbled. There was a new connection between us. As new age as it sounds, there was a oneness. There was complete trust. And now that we've developed this trust, we're free to play and try new things without fear of recrimination. We don't have all the inhibitions and reservations we had before. We've taken our relationship to a higher plane.

C: A lot of things. Seeing women squirt and writhe and go crazy with the pleasure. Feeling them get so wet and tight as they convulse against your finger. It really boosts a man's self-confidence. You don't have to wonder if you're better in bed than the last guy she was with, you know? Unless he knows this technique, you know you're better. And you can usually tell right away, afterwards.

Did your lover know she could ejaculate?

A: No. She was stunned afterwards.

B: Are you kidding? She couldn't believe it. I had to show her the book to convince her that she hadn't lost control and wet the bed.

C: Mostly no.

How much fluid does your lover normally produce when she ejaculates?

A: If you want an average, I'd guess she produces somewhere between a tablespoon full and half a cup. Although the first time, it seemed like at least a cupful, maybe more.

To be honest I haven't found any rhyme or reason to the amount she ejaculates. Sometimes the fluid gushes out of her and other times it's little more than a trickle and hardly noticeable. It doesn't seem to coincide with the intensity of her orgasm, either.

You know, I guess the same is true with men if you think about it. I mean, the amount varies and the projection varies. Sometimes we can shoot for two or three feet while other times the sperm just spurts out of us.

B: The first time I did it to her, it was a lot. We didn't measure it, but she drenched the bed so much that we had to change the sheets. Since then, the amount has varied. Some nights she really drenches the bed and some nights it just kind of oozes out of her.

C: Women put men to shame. They say that men usually make about a teaspoonful of sperm. But most of the women I've tried this technique on drench the bed. I'd say it's usually a cupful.

What other comments can you share with us?

A: I'm still in awe of the G-Spot. It amazes me that I've been sexually active for 21 years now—since I was 17—yet I never found the G-Spot. Considering that I had several girlfriends before I got married, plus 15 years of marriage and having sex 2 or 3 times a week, it just boggles my mind that I—we— never came across it! And now that I know it exists, it's almost embarrassing to think that it's been there all along. It's incredible because I can see how I could have passed through my whole life without ever knowing about it, had you not shared your information in this book.

B: Your technique has changed my life and my marriage for the better. Thank you. You don't know what a difference you've made in mine and my wife's lives.

C: I wish you would stop selling this book so other guys wouldn't find out about it.

The Ending Climax

Pat yourself on the back. Whether or not your first attempt at the G-Spot orgasm is successful, you've done two great things. You've spent a little time and money to unselfishly help your partner feel the ultimate in female pleasure, a noble act indeed. And you've made an investment in yourself, gaining knowledge that you can carry throughout life, knowledge that can be used time-and-time again to deliver the ultimate in female orgasms.

Voluntary Questionnaire:

Part 1

A Study of the G-Spot

To aid us and your partner in making strides in G-Spot orgasms, we encourage all readers to complete the following survey or mail any personal comments or questions. Mail should be directed to:

Donald L. Hicks

P. O. Box 734

Powhatan, Virginia, 23139

Part 1

***(To Be Filled Out By the Person
Who "Applied" the G-Spot Stimulation)***

Your age: ___   Your sex: ___

Race: -White   -Asian -Native American

       -Black -Hispanic   -Other_____

1. Did you read the entire book?
   -Yes
   -No If you answered "No", which part did you not read,
   and why?_____

   _____

2. What was the most extraordinary or remarkable thing you
   learned from this book?_____

   _____

3. Before reading the book, were you aware of the
   G-Spot's location?   -Yes   -No

4. Were you aware that females can ejaculate?   -Yes   -No

5. Did you find the book easy to follow? -Yes   -No

6. Can you suggest any way to improve this book? -Yes   -No If
   so, how?_____

7. Was your first attempt at applying the G-Spot orgasm success-
   ful? -Yes   -No
   If not, how many attempts were made before you succeeded? ____
   Did you eventually succeed? -Yes   -No

8. If you succeeded (on any attempt), did your lover ejaculate? - Yes -No

9. If your lover ejaculated, how much fluid did she produce? -A Trickle -About a teaspoonful -A Tablespoonful -A cup -She drenched the bed sheets

9. Approximately how long did it take from the beginning of actual G-Spot stimulation until the orgasm began?
_____ Hours _____ Minutes.

10. Approximately how long did the orgasm last? ___ Minutes

11. Was your lover surprised by the intensity of the orgasm?
-Yes -No

12. Was your lover surprised to learn she could ejaculate?
-Yes -No

13. Which of the following choices best matches your lover's reaction after the orgasm? (Choose up to three).
—Joyous/Elated   —Thankful
— "Lovy"/Romantic   —Frustrated
—Embarrassed   —Shy
—Ready for more   —Satiated/Fulfilled
—Surprised   —Angry
—Curious   —Other:_____

What other comments can you share with us?

_____

_____

_____

_____

Part 2

(This section is to be completed by the female who received the G-Spot stimulation)

Your age: _____

Race: -White -Asian -Native American
         -Black -Hispanic   -Other_____

1. Do you typically orgasm during foreplay and/or intercourse? -Yes -No

2. If you typically orgasm, how many times do you normally orgasm (on average) during intercourse (foreplay included)?
   - 0 to 1   - 2 to 3 - 4 to 5 - 5 or more

3. How long is your average orgasm?
   - Average (8 to 19 seconds) ___ Seconds   -Unknown

4. What do you feel is the most predominant source of
   your orgasms?   -Clitoral Stimulation
                        -Originating from the vagina
                        -Other:_____

5. Did you experience a "G-Spot" orgasm when your partner applied this technique? -Yes -No

6. If yes, how did you feel afterwards?

—Joyous/Elated   —Thankful

— "Lovy"/Romantic   —Frustrated

—Embarrassed   —Shy

—Ready for more   —Satiated/Fulfilled

—Surprised   —Angry

—Curious   —Other:_____

7. Did you ejaculate?   -Yes   -No

8. Prior to the ejaculation, did you know females have the ability to ejaculate? -Yes   -No

9. How did this orgasm compare to previous orgasms you've had?

_____

_____

10. Was there anything you did not like about the G-Spot orgasm or the technique your lover used?

_____

_____

11. What other comments can you share?

_____

_____

_____

_____

_____

12. On a scale of "1 to 10" with "1" being least pleasurable and "10" being most pleasurable, how would rate orgasms you've experienced from the following.
(use "0" if never experienced)

A: Clitoral Stimulation ___

B: Vaginal Stimulation ___

C: G-Spot Stimulation ___

All comments gathered through this survey become the property of Hooked on Books. Hooked on Books shall not use any names or other information that disclose the identities of the individuals in the survey.

Optional Disclosure

Name: _____

Email Address: _____

Address: _____

City: _____

State: _____

Zip: _____

Country: _____

Resources for Further Research

Reading Materials

Highly Recommended Reading:

The G Spot and Other Discoveries About Human Sexuality
by Alice Kahn Ladas, Beverly Whipple, and John Perry (1982)
Dell Publishing
A Div. Of Bantam Doubleday Dell Publishing Group. , Inc.

Other Recommended Reading:

The Hite Report: A Nationwide Study on Female Sexuality
by Shere Hite (1976)
Dell Publishing Co. , Inc.

The G-Spot in Words and Pictures (1988)
by Feliz G. Berger
Orion-Verlag

Secrets to Sensual Lovemaking: The Ultimate in Female Ecstasy
by Tom Leonardi (1998)
Signet
Published by the Penguin Group

Web Sites

1. Sexual Health.com - http://www.sexhealth.com
   This site is a great information resource. It allows visitors to
   ask questions, browse topics, videos, and products. It also has a
   board of sexual "experts".

2. Women.com - http://www.women.com
   Women.com has a host of channels (including a sex channel
   and a health channel) and both articles and information available
   regarding women's health, interests, and sexuality. There is a
   great deal of focus on Orgasm and "The Moan Zone", "Great
   Vibes", etc... It also has links to Redbook, Cosmopolitan, and
   eHarlquin (for more of the same).

3. The Kinsey Institute - http://www.indiana.edu/~kinsey
   The Kinsey Institute has a host of research publications available,
   along with upcoming events and sexology links.

4. The American Association of Sex Educators, Counselors, and
   Therapists (AASECT) - http://www.aasect.org/about.cfm
   A non-profit professional organization of sexuality educators,
   sex counselors and sex therapists, AASECT members include
   physicians, nurses, social workers, psychologists, allied health
   professionals, clergy members, lawyers, sociologists, marriage
   and family counselors and therapists, family planning specialists
   and researchers, as well as students in relevant professional
   disciplines. These individuals share an interest in promoting
   understanding of human sexuality and healthy sexual behavior.

5. Lover's Lane® - http://www.loverslane.com
   Lover's Lane is a tasteful adult resource, geared toward couples.
   They offer adult books, apparel, and sex toys.

Key Words Glossary

A

analgesic An agent for producing insensibility to pain.

anterior Located in the front; the front wall.

B

blended orgasm Multiple orgasms occurring simultaneously.

bonding The act of growing emotionally united.

C

climax The highest point; orgasm.

clitoris A small, highly sensitive organ at the anterior or ventral part of the vulva, homologous to the penis.

D, E, F

elucidate To make clear by explanation; to bring to light.

female ejaculation The expulsion of liquid from the urethra.

female prostate Also known as the Skene Glands or paraurethral glands; A network of glands and ducts surrounding the urethra and bladder neck.

G

G-Spot The Gräfenburg Spot. A highly sensitive area located on the anterior wall of the vagina. This spot was named by Dr. Beverly Whipple and Dr. John Perry, after Dr. Ernst Gräfenburg.

G-Spot virgin A woman who has never experienced a G-Spot orgasm.

ghost sensation A false sensation; in the context of this book, a false feeling of the need to urinate.

Goal Seeker Individuals who focus on achieving orgasm each sexual experience and are discontent if orgasm does not occur.

gynecologists Doctors specializing in diseases and hygiene of women.

H

hovering Floating; to be in an uncertain state. In the context of this book, to hold the hand above sensitive areas of the partner's body to create sexual anxiety.

hypothesize An assumption made in order to test it's validity.

I

immunohistochemical Of or relating to the application of histochemical and immunologic methods to chemical analysis of living cells and tissues.

innervate To supply with nerves; to arouse or stimulate (a nerve or an organ) to activity.

introitis The first part of a mass; often the opening.

J, K

kachapati A rite of passage reportedly practiced by the Batoro tribe of Africa, through which adolescent girls were taught to "spray the walls" and thus graduate into a state of nubility.

Kegel exercises Exercises designed to strengthen the pubococcygeus muscles.

L

labia Folds of fatty or vascular flesh bounding the vulva; the lips; often broken down into the Labia Majora (outer folds) and Labia Minora (inner folds).

M

magic triangle The area of the genitals covered in pubic hair.

monolithic A social structure exhibiting solid uniformity.

N, O

obstetricians Physicians who specialize in pregnancy and childbirth.

orgasm A climax during sexual excitement.

Orgasm Anxiety A condition characterized by chronic fear of not attaining orgasm during intercourse.

P

paraurethral Adjacent to the urethra.

Performance Givers Persons feeling the need to orgasm for the benefit of their sexual partner.

physiological The science dealing with functions of living matter or beings; the functional processes in an organism or any of its parts.

pubococcygeus muscle A muscle group that acts to help support the pelvic viscera, to draw the lower end of the rectum toward the pubis, and to constrict the rectum and female vagina.

Q, R

retrograde ejaculation In the context of this work, the occurrence of fluids ejaculating backward into the bladder instead of being outwardly expelled from the urethra.

S, T

safer sex Practices minimizing contact with bodily fluids or reducing the risk of contracting sexually transmitted disease.

sexual response Response to sexual stimulus.

Skene's glands A small mass of glands and ducts surrounding the urethra; often considered as the female prostate glands or paraurethral glands..

stimulation To arouse, excite, or make more active.

U

urethra The canal that carries urine (to egress) from the bladder; also serving as a passageway for the ejection of male and female ejaculate.

USI Urinary Stress Incontinence. The loss of control or restraint of the bladder.

uterus The womb; An organ of the female for containing and developing fetuses.

V - Z

vaginal marksman A sexual partner who's goal is to initiate vaginal stimulation upon the first permissible opportunity, often in haste.

vulva The external genital parts of the female.

About the Author

Donald L. Hicks

Donald Hicks is the author of three novels, numerous newspaper and magazine articles, and award-winning poetry. He attended Southern State Community College and is a devoted researcher of human sexuality and intra-couple relationships.

Together with their dog and cat, Donald and his wife of 20 years live on a rolling farm in rural Virginia. They are both currently working on new novels.

Materials Used in Preparing This Guide

Bibliography

The G Spot and Other Discoveries About Human Sexuality
by Alice Kahn Ladas, Beverly Whipple, and John Perry (1982)
Dell Publishing
A Div. Of Bantam Doubleday Dell Publishing Group. , Inc.

The Hite Report: A Nationwide Study on Female Sexuality
by Shere Hite (1976)
Dell Publishing Co. , Inc.

The G-Spot in Words and Pictures (1988)
by Feliz G. Berger
Orion-Verlag

Secrets to Sensual Lovemaking: The Ultimate in Female Ecstasy
by Tom Leonardi (1998)
Signet
Published by the Penguin Group

Endnotes

[i] Stoff, J. A., M.D., and Clouatre, D., Ph.D.: *The Prostate Miracle, New Natural Therapies That Can Save Your Life*; Kensington Pub. Corp.; 2000

[ii] Whipple, B., Ph.D., RN, FAAN, and Komisaurak, B. R., Ph.D.: *Beyond the G Spot: Recent Research on Female Sexuality*; Psychiatric Annals 29:1, pgs 35-57; January, 1999

[iii] Singer, I,: *The Goals of Human Sexuality*; Norton, New York, 1973 — and/or — Singer, J., and Singer, I.: *Types of Female Orgasm*; The Journal of Sex Research, 8; 1972

[iv] Ladas, A., Whipple, B., and Perry, J.: *The G Spot and Other Discoveries about Human Sexuality*; Dell Publishing, pgs 140-154; 1982

[v] Hite, S.,: *The Hite Report*; Dell Publishing, pg. 618; 1976

[vi] Ogden G.: *Perceptions of Touch in Easily Orgasmic Women During Peak Sexual Experiences;* San Francisco, Institute for Advanced Study of Human Sexuality; 1981. Doctoral Dissertation.

[vii] Whipple, B., Ogden, G., and Komisaruk, B. R.: *Physiological Correlates of Imagery Induced Orgasm in Women;* Arch. Sexual Behavior, 21(2):121-133; 1992

[viii] Ladas, A., Whipple, B., and Perry, J.: The G Spot and Other Discoveries about Human Sexuality; Dell Publishing, pgs 70-71; 1982

[ix] Addiego, F., Belzer, E. G., Comolli, J., et al.; *Female Ejaculation: A Case Study;* The Journal of Sex Research, 17:31-21; 1981

[x] Zaviacic, M., Dolezalova, S., Holoman, I. K., et al: *Concentrations of fructose in female ejaculate and urine: A Comparative Biochemical Study;* The Journal of Sex Research, 24: 319-325; 1988

[xi] Belzer, E. G., Whipple, B., Moger, W.: *On Female Ejaculation;* The Journal of Sex Research, 20: 403-406; 1984

[xii] Sensabaugh, G. R., Kahane, D.: *Biochemical Studies on "Female Ejaculates"*. Presented at the meeting of the California Association of Criminologists, Newport Beach, CA; May, 1982

[xiii] Zaviacic, M., Whipple, B.: *Update on the Female Prostate and the Phenomenon of Female Ejaculation;* The Journal of Sex Research: Vol

30, No 2, pgs 148-121; 1993

[xiv] Ladas, A., Whipple, B., and Perry, J.: *The G Spot and Other Discoveries about Human Sexuality*; Dell Publishing; 1982

[xv] Addiego, F., Belzer, E. G., Comolli, J., et al.: *Female Ejaculation: A Case Study;* The Journal of Sex Research, 17: 13-21; 1981

[xvi] Leonardi, T.: *Secrets of Sensual Lovemaking, The Ultimate in Female Ecstasy;* Signet, pgs 101-103; 1998

[xvii] Ladas, A., Whipple, B., and Perry, J.: *The G Spot and Other Discoveries about Human Sexuality*; Dell Publishing, pg 81; 1982

[xviii] Cabello Santamaria, F.: *Female Ejaculation, Myth or Reality;* in J. J. Borras-Valls & M. Perez-Conchillo (Eds). Sexuality and Human Rights: Proceedings of the XIII World Congress of Sexology, Valencia, NAU llibres., pgs 325-333; 1998

[xix] Zaviacic, M., Zaviacicova, A., Holoman, I. K., and Molcan, J.: *Female urethral expulsions evoked by local digital stimulation of the G Spot: Differences in the response patterns;* The Journal of Sex Research 24: 311-318; 1988

[xx] Ladas, A., Whipple, B., and Perry, J.: *The G Spot and Other Discoveries about Human Sexuality*; Dell Publishing, pg 69; 1982

[xxi] As stated per Ladas, A., Whipple, B., and Perry, J.: *The G Spot and Other Discoveries about Human Sexuality*; Dell Publishing (1982), pg 75, shown as reference #4 involving a personal communication by Phil Kilbraten, anthropologist; Bryn Mawr College, April 26, 1980

[xxii] Muller, J., et al; *The Myocardial Onset Study;* The Journal of the American Medical Association; May, 1996

[xxiii] Whipple, B.: *Sexual counseling of couples after a mastectomy or myocardial infraction*; Nurs Forum, 23: 85-91; 1987/88

[xxiv] de Graaf, R.: *New Treatise Concerning the Generative Organs of Women; Journal of Reproduction and Fertility*, H.B. Jocelyn and B. P. Setchell, (eds), Oxford, England, pgs 103-107; 1672

[xxv] Gräfenburg, E., and Dickinson, R.: *Conception Control by Plastic Cervix Cap,:*pgs 337-338, 1950

[xxvi] URL = http://www.indiana.edu/~kisiss/topten.html; The Kinsey Institute for Research in Sex, Gender, and Reproduction, Inc.: 1998-2000

Printed in the United States
20112LVS00001B/187